THE
WIDE WORLD OF
CODING

The People and Careers
behind the Programs

JENNIFER CONNOR-SMITH

TFCB

TWENTY-FIRST CENTURY BOOKS / MINNEAPOLIS

To Casey, Celia, Mallory, and all the inspirational people using code to build a better world

ACKNOWLEDGMENTS
Thank you to all the people and organizations dedicated to opening doors for the next generation of developers.

A special thank-you to Casey Smith, who has double-checked my work, answered every coding-related question I've asked, and volunteered himself into creating custom apps that make my work easier.

Twenty-First Century Books™
An imprint of Lerner Publishing Group, Inc.
241 First Avenue North
Minneapolis, MN 55401 USA

For reading levels and more information, look up this title at www.lernerbooks.com.

Main body text set in Adrianna Condensed.
Typeface provided by Chank.

Library of Congress Cataloging-in-Publication Data

Names: Connor-Smith, Jennifer, 1972– author.
Title: The wide world of coding : the people and careers behind the programs / by Jennifer Connor-Smith.
Description: Minneapolis, MN : Twenty-First Century Books, [2020] | Includes bibliographical references and index. | Audience: Age 12–18. | Audience: Grades 9–12. |
Identifiers: LCCN 2019009071 (print) | LCCN 2019012439 (ebook) |
     ISBN 9781541580909 (eb pdf) | ISBN 9781541552821 (lb : alk. paper)
Subjects: LCSH: Computer programming—Vocational guidance—Juvenile literature. | Computer programmers—Juvenile literature.
Classification: LCC QA76.25 (ebook) | LCC QA76.25 .C566 2020 (print) | DDC 005.1023—dc23

LC record available at https://lccn.loc.gov/2019009071

Manufactured in the United States of America
1-45658-41685-10/9/2019

CONTENTS

INTRODUCTION

In summer 2014, high school students Andrea (Andy) Gonzales and Sophie Houser met at a Girls Who Code immersion program in New York City. Andy came with basic coding skills, but Sophie had no idea what she was getting into. She knew coding involved a language, but wondered, "Was it letters or numbers or a mixture of both? Did you do it in a Google doc, or did you need a special program to code?" She had struggled with learning Spanish in school and wanted to know, "Would I have to make flash cards and memorize coding nouns and coding verbs and coding tenses?"

A few weeks later, Sophie had a handle on several programming languages— no flash cards required—and was ready to partner with Andy to build an app. As they tossed around ideas, Andy complained about video games featuring scantily clad female characters and gory deaths. The pair realized how strange it is that people accept bloody video games but freak out about women getting their periods.

Frustrated by the taboo around menstruation, Sophie and Andy decided to make both a game and a point. To bolster their case, they collected stories about period-related stigma. Many were frustrating, such as girls in India missing school because they lacked crucial supplies. Others were amusing, such as when Texas officials allowed guns into the Texas State Capitol but confiscated wrapped tampons they feared women might throw in protest.

Sophie and Andy's vision for *Tampon Run* came together quickly. Players would pelt enemies with tampons and reload by leaping for tampon boxes. Coding the game took much longer. Sophie thought it would only take an hour to make their character jump, but a morning of troubleshooting stretched through the afternoon. By the end of the day, she hated her immobile character, her code, her computer, and her lack of coding skills. Finally, while preparing to bike home, she realized her

Sophie Houser (*left*) and Andrea Gonzales attend the Tribeca Disruptive Innovation Awards at the 2015 Tribeca Film Festival in New York City.

character was simply jumping too quickly for anyone to see—an easy problem to fix. Andy had a similar experience. She thought getting their character to run would be easy, but ended up watching online tutorials and wrestling with the code until three in the morning.

After weeks of coding, Sophie and Andy braced themselves to share the game with an audience of families and tech mentors. Sophie dreaded public speaking and didn't want to talk about tampons, or anything else, in front of a crowd. Andy feared her conservative parents would disapprove of a tampon-throwing game entirely.

As it turned out, neither needed to worry. Sophie forgot her lines but read her note card to enthusiastic applause. Andy's parents simply admired her hard work.

Buoyed by their success, Sophie and Andy shared the game online. To their surprise, *Tampon Run* went viral, attracting coverage from media companies such as CNN, BuzzFeed, and *Teen Vogue* and winning a Webby People's Voice Award. Sophie and Andy worked with the tech company Pivotal Labs to produce an iPhone version of the game, spoke at TEDx, and wrote a book, *Girl Code: Gaming, Going Viral, and Getting It Done.*

When Sophie was asked to describe her superpower, at first, she couldn't think of an answer. She didn't have any special skills—she just tried hard. Suddenly, she realized trying hard was her superpower, saying, "When I set a goal for myself, I do whatever it takes to achieve it, even when it feels like an impossible challenge at first." With those simple words, Sophie captured the magic of succeeding as a software developer.

Coding doesn't take a genius-level IQ or an obsession with technology, just a willingness to keep moving forward, one step at a time.

After graduating from high school, Sophie and Andy both kept moving forward. Andy majored in computer science at the University of North Carolina–Chapel Hill and interned at Microsoft. Sophie majored in computer science at Brown University and interned with Facebook. They also had plenty of time to explore other interests. Andy produced podcasts and volunteered with people living in supportive housing. Sophie ran engineering clubs for elementary school students and taught sex education classes.

Unlike Sophie and Andy, most developers won't get national attention for their work. But the girls' story reflects many stories from those who enter the field of software development. People from all different backgrounds, with a wide range of interests, become developers. Like Sophie, many start out feeling a bit intimidated before discovering how easy coding can be.

In 2018 over 22 million people around the world worked as software developers. Despite stereotypes portraying developers as brilliant, coding-obsessed nerds, developers are ordinary people who spend their free time hanging out with friends and family, watching TV, volunteering, creating art, or playing sports.

Many coding books teach people how to use specific programming languages. Learning such languages is obviously important, but coding is about much more than typing commands. This book focuses on how software developers think and why their work matters. The first half covers the process of turning an idea into an app, from choosing a programming language to chasing down coding errors. It reveals how developers tackle complex ideas, manage floods of data, and train artificial intelligence programs. These ideas will be easier to follow if you read the first four chapters in order.

You can read the second half of the book, which focuses on social and ethical issues, in any order. Chapters 5 through 8 explore how tech companies make money by exploiting human psychology, ways developers accidentally create discriminatory artificial intelligence programs, and how diversity in tech leads to better code. By the end of this book, you will see that coding isn't about memorizing a set of obscure commands—it is about shaping the world we live in.

CHAPTER 1

DIVING INTO DEVELOPMENT

Careers in software development take many forms. Some people enter the field because they love math, science, and high-tech gadgets. Others become developers because they love creative work or want to solve a social problem. Some developers spend much of their time writing code. Others focus on managing teams or making apps more user-friendly. Because software development careers offer great flexibility, people often begin in one role and transition to another as they discover the work they love most.

A DEVELOPER BY ANY OTHER NAME

People who create software go by many names, including computer programmer, software developer, software engineer, and coder. Often people shorten those terms to programmer, developer, or dev. Just as mechanical engineers use steel and concrete to construct bridges, software engineers use units of code to build programs.

Software development is such a broad field that any two developers are likely to work on very different projects and have different day-to-day responsibilities. One developer might use advanced math to build powerful encryption tools for the CIA, while another builds a child-friendly app to help kindergartners manage diabetes.

Developers also work in many different environments. Some work for software-focused companies such as Google or Microsoft, producing programs millions of people will use. Others work for large organizations that rely on customized software, such as hospitals, universities, airports, or manufacturers. Some developers work in the entertainment industry, creating video games or movie special effects. Still others work as consultants, writing code for small businesses that don't need full-time developers. A few developers work independently, creating and marketing their own apps.

Developers can also take on very different roles. Systems programmers create and improve operating systems. Their code helps devices work well, so smartphone users can simultaneously stream music, search the web, and receive texts. Software architects focus on the big-picture design of programs, creating blueprints for other developers to follow. Front-end developers work on the parts of programs users see, while back-end developers build the underlying components.

Regardless of a developer's role or environment, the work offers opportunities for creative problem-solving and teamwork.

BECOMING A DEVELOPER

You might think that learning to code requires a perfect GPA, but it's really more about being patient, persistent, and creative. Many successful developers struggled with math or science in school. Although some started coding as kids, others didn't write a line of code until after their own kids left home.

Many developers get into the field by studying computer science in college. Most colleges and universities offer a basic computer science, software development, or software engineering major. Some offer specialized degrees, such as game design or information systems security. These degrees can open doors: about half of all job advertisements for developers list a coding-related degree as a requirement or preference.

However, not all coding-related jobs require a college degree. If people have great coding skills, many employers don't care where they got them. Steve Jobs and Steve Wozniak, the founders of Apple Computer, dropped out of college and learned by doing. So did Mark Zuckerberg,

Apple cofounder Steve Jobs announces new iPhone software at an event in 2010.

founder of Facebook, and Bill Gates and Paul Allen, founders of Microsoft. Around the world, only about 43 percent of developers have a coding-related degree.

Instead of getting a college degree, many people learn to code by enrolling in coding boot camps, intensive programs that teach basic skills in just a few months. Tuition averages about $12,000, but many boot camps offer scholarships or allow students to start paying off the tuition costs after they get a coding job. Most are for people ages 18 and older, since the goal is for graduates to move straight into full-time work.

Mark Zuckerberg started Facebook with his roommates from their dorm room at Harvard University. He dropped out his sophomore year to work on the website.

People of all ages can also learn to code without spending any money at all. Massive open online classes are free, web-based classes. Many allow people of any age to sign up, while others require students to be at least 13 years old. Tech companies and colleges offer these classes ranging from app development to data management. Some courses are for beginners. Others are intended for people with several years of coding experience. These classes work best for students motivated enough to do the assigned homework, even when they know they won't be getting a grade.

Independent learners can also teach themselves to code using books and free online tutorials (see suggested websites in the back of the book). Public libraries have many learn-to-code books written for children and teenagers. Some focus on helping students learn a specific programming language. Others teach the basics of animation or game design.

Online, aspiring coders can find resources for every age and experience level, from kindergartners designing cartoon characters to adults developing marketable apps. Teenagers can use these free online resources to make real programs, such as the middle school girls in Texas who used the MIT App Inventor website to build an app that helps blind students find their way around the school building.

Students who prefer real-life communities to virtual ones can learn to code through classes at school, in clubs, or at coding camps. Organizations such as CoderDojo (CoderDojo.com), Code Club (CodeClubWorld.org), and Girls Who Code (GirlsWhoCode.com) run free coding clubs for children and teenagers around the world. Many of the coding camps that cost money offer scholarships for students.

With all of these resources, anyone who wants to learn to code can start today, regardless of age or ability to pay for classes.

COMPUTATIONAL THINKING

Compared to the speed and accuracy of computers, humans fall terribly short—a pocket-sized iPhone 11 can handle a whopping 1 trillion operations per second. However, despite their speed, computers are not smart and cannot think or reason. Unlike humans, they cannot even carry out a simple task without very specific instructions. Toddlers can easily follow a direction such as "Go get your ball." For a robot to follow that direction, it would first need a human to write hundreds of thousands of lines of code describing how to detect the ball, chart a path to the ball, move forward, orient its hand, grasp the ball, and so on.

When writing programs, a software developer's main job is identifying the series of steps required to accomplish a task. Developers call this computational thinking, which involves the following:

» decomposition—breaking complicated problems into several smaller, simpler problems

» pattern recognition—identifying similarities across problems

» abstraction—distinguishing between essential and nonessential parts of problems

» designing algorithms—creating a set of step-by-step directions to solve problems

Computational thinking may sound daunting, but people do it all the time. Imagine you want to go to the movies with friends. To get there you need to solve many smaller problems—picking the movie, getting permission to go, and finding a way there (decomposition). If you usually have to finish chores before having a friend over, you can predict that rule applies to going to see movies too (pattern recognition). Getting to the movie is essential, but the method of travel—walking, taking the bus, or having a parent drive—is not (abstraction). You will need to solve problems in the right order, such as picking the location before choosing a bus route and borrowing money before buying a ticket (designing algorithms).

Computational thinking is so central to software development that many learn-to-code apps emphasize it over writing code. With Microsoft's Kodu Game Lab, people don't even need a keyboard to fill a game world with obstacles and point-earning challenges. The drag-and-drop interface focuses on logical thinking, not the details of programming languages.

ACTIVITY: OUTLINE A PROGRAM

Before developers write code, they identify every step the program needs to carry out. To get a feel for this, list every step required for a door-opening robot to let your friends into the house after they ring the doorbell.

A door-opening robot needs to do the following:

- recognize the sound of the doorbell
- map a route to the door
- identify and avoid obstacles
- grasp and operate the deadbolt and doorknob
- move backward while opening the door
- identify the people at the door as friends or annoying salespeople
- keep salespeople out but let friends in
- determine whether all friends on the doorstep have entered
- close and lock the door after all friends have entered

Those steps need even more detail. To turn the doorknob, the robot must do the following:

- identify the doorknob
- orient its hand to align with the doorknob
- close its hand with enough pressure to turn the knob without damaging it
- rotate its hand the correct amount
- hold that rotation while pulling the door open . . .

TYPES OF SOFTWARE

Any program giving instructions to a computer, tablet, phone, game console, or electronic device counts as software. Software comes in three main types:

Operating systems. Every computer needs an operating system (OS) to manage such basic functions as storing information, accepting inputs, and displaying information. Different devices need different operating systems. Most personal computers run Windows OS, but Apple computers run macOS. Web servers, which handle websites and online programs, typically run Linux OS. Almost all smartphones run Google's Android OS, with the exception of iPhones, which run iOS.

Applications. All other software running on personal computers, mobile devices, or websites counts as an application, also called an app or program. Video games, word processors, Instagram, and Snapchat are all apps. So are the programs guiding space probes and controlling assembly-line robots.

Embedded software. Embedded software, also called firmware, controls electronic devices such as DVD players, washing machines, talking toys, and internet-connected "smart" devices such as fitness trackers. When a microwave runs the popcorn setting, its firmware uses data from steam-monitoring sensors to decide when to turn off. Without firmware, digital cameras wouldn't focus, traffic lights would stay red, and elevators wouldn't move.

SOFTWARE DEVELOPMENT: NOT JUST FOR CODERS

Creating high-quality software requires a team of people with diverse skill sets. Many team members never write a single line of code.

System administrators (sysadmins) and network engineers make sure developers have the software and computer setups they need for their work. Sysadmins install and update software, manage email systems, and back up crucial data. Network engineers configure systems so information flows quickly and reliably between computers. Their work includes troubleshooting outages and installing firewalls to keep hackers out of the system.

Program managers keep companies on track by coordinating multiple, related projects. For example, a company may plan to design new animation software and use that software to create several video games—a series of projects that may take years to complete. To achieve its goal, the company will need teams working on everything from character creation to marketing plans. Program managers keep the whole set of projects on track by organizing teams, making budget decisions, and setting long-term goals.

Project managers transform long-term goals into detailed to-do lists. They estimate the time needed to complete tasks, assign work, track progress, and monitor spending. When problems inevitably arise, project managers juggle deadlines or spread work across more teams. They keep everyone organized with Gantt charts, or elaborate color-coded displays of tasks and timelines. Some project managers have computer science backgrounds, but many come from the business world.

Business analysts translate between developers and clients who don't have programming backgrounds. For example, a solar panel company may want to create an app that allows homeowners to see how much energy their rooftop solar panels generate each day. The company knows what the software should do, but not how to create it. Business analysts would document the solar company's needs and produce a clear set of requirements for developers, who then go on to create the app for the solar panel company.

Quality assurance (QA) specialists seek out bugs (software problems) that keep programs from working well. They also try to trip up software by making every mistake and bad decision they can dream up. Their work ensures a program will be able to handle whatever users throw at it.

User experience (UX) and **user interface (UI)** designers make software fun and easy to use. UX designers simplify human-computer interactions by making it obvious how to complete tasks. Their work includes everything from designing the sign-up process for online games to making information easy to find on drop-down menus. UX designers also protect users from themselves—for example, by forcing users to click through an extra "Yes, delete files permanently" step to keep them from accidentally erasing files.

UI designers focus on the parts of programs users see, creating attractive screens with a consistent look and feel. They design interactive elements, such as clickable buttons, and use the size, color, and placement of those elements to grab users' attention and guide their actions. UX and UI designers may have psychology, computer science, or visual design backgrounds.

Graphic designers create images and icons, choose color palettes, and design page layouts. Their work often overlaps with that of UX and UI designers. Sometimes the same people fill these roles on a project. The graphic designers' work determines whether an app looks serious, elegant, edgy, or fun.

Technical writers, trainers, and technical support staff bridge the gap between software developers and software users. Technical writers create instruction

BRINGING VIDEO GAMES TO LIFE

The gaming industry is a financial powerhouse—consumers spent $43 billion on games and hardware in 2018 alone. All of that money pouring in means companies can hire huge teams, such as the nearly 700 people Epic Games had working on *Fortnite* in 2018. So many people worked on *Call of Duty: WWII* that it takes eight minutes for the list of developers to scroll up the screen during the credits.

Developers who write the code underlying video games are called game engineers. On large teams, game engineers often take on specialized roles. Artificial intelligence programmers craft realistic computer-controlled characters. Physics programmers code falls, collisions, and billowing smoke. Level editors use code, art, and sounds created by others to create unique game levels. User interface programmers design maps, displays, and status indicators to help players navigate the game world. Network programmers write the code allowing thousands of people to play together online.

Technically oriented developers may create game engines—the software other developers use to control nonplayer characters, handle collisions, and add sound effects. Or they may develop animation software that allows artists to add light, shadow, and texture to objects.

Game design studios also have non-coding roles. Producers oversee every aspect of game production, from supervising teams to managing budgets. Creative directors manage the writers, artists, audio engineers, and musicians who bring the game world to life. Quality assurance teams seek out glitches, putting them among the lucky few people in the world who get paid to play video games.

manuals, write help function text, and create frequently asked question (FAQ) pages. Trainers help users become experts at programs and apps. Some create online tutorials, while others travel the country as consultants. Most technical writers and trainers don't have a programming background—social and communication skills matter more. Trainers who do have a computer science background may specialize in working with developers, teaching them how to get the most out of a programming languages or software development tool.

Technical support staff step in when users get lost, helping users make sense of software through phone calls, emails, or online chats. This job requires patience and strong problem-solving skills because the problem could lie with the software itself or

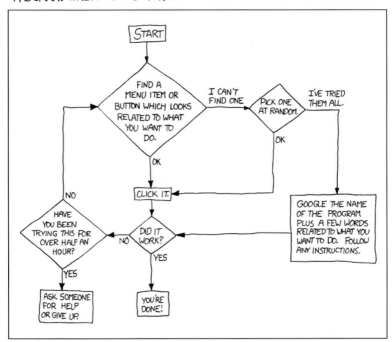

This *XKCD* comic pokes fun at the tech support process.

with the person using it. Users may be trying to do something the software can't do, missing a crucial step, or just bewildered by computers. Tech support teams privately use acronyms such as PICNIC (Problem In Chair, Not In Computer), to describe problems caused by users rather than by the software. Often tech support discovers the solution is as simple as rebooting a computer. Other times, tech support discovers bugs developers will need to fix in the next update.

These are just a few of the jobs related to software development. Because software has become so widespread, almost any profession can be linked to software

SOFTWARE DEVELOPMENT SALARIES

Strong demand for software translates to high salaries and low unemployment rates. These salaries reflect the income people might reach in the middle of their career.

JOB TITLE	AVERAGE ANNUAL SALARY (UNITED STATES, IN DOLLARS)
Software developer	107,000
Systems administrator	86,000
Network engineer	108,000
Program manager	131,000
Project manager	85,000
Business analyst	74,000
Quality assurance engineer	74,000
User experience designer	83,000
User interface designer	73,000
Graphic designer	50,000
Technical writer	66,000
Technical support	54,000
Software trainer	60,000

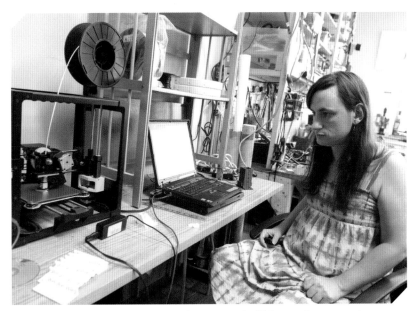

A member of HacDC uses a 3D printer. Hackerspaces, or hacklabs, are often community-run, nonprofit spaces where developers and creatives can socialize and collaborate on projects.

development. For example, lawyers help developers protect their intellectual property and policy makers help regulate privacy online. Whatever a person's interests, they can find a place in the world of software development.

WHY CODE?

Some people become developers because they love the creative challenges and the thrill of inventing something new. Because technology changes quickly, the job never gets stale—developers always have new tools to explore and new skills to learn. Other people choose software development careers for the excellent salaries and job security.

Because these careers are in high demand, jobs are easy to find in most parts of the country. Most software development jobs also offer flexible schedules, good work-life balance, and perks such as working from home or wearing jeans to the office. They also allow people to work in fields related to their hobbies. Not many kids grow up to be astronauts or esports stars, but they can become programmers who write code for NASA or create video games for a living.

Some people become developers so that they can be creative problem solvers.

Many developers never intended to become programmers. Instead, they set out to create safe communities or improve schools and discovered software was the tool they needed to make the world a better place. Code the Change, founded by Stanford University, pairs computer science students with nonprofits to solve social problems. The founders realized that most social change organizations needed more technical resources, but few student activists had explored computer science careers. In the last few years, Code the Change groups around the country have created apps to monitor child malnutrition in Guatemala and track crop disease in Uganda. Groups have also developed apps to log search-and-rescue data in the field, connect domestic violence survivors with shelter space, and keep college students safe when walking home at night.

Whether a person loves diving into the latest technology or supporting animal shelters, software development jobs will allow them to earn a good living while following their passion.

CHAPTER 2

BRINGING PROGRAMS TO LIFE

I n 1988 the Soviet Union (a group of republics that included Russia) launched the *Phobos 1* and *Phobos 2* probes to explore Phobos, an irregularly shaped moon orbiting Mars. Before launch, the Moscow and Yevpatoriya space centers argued about which center should have mission control. Ultimately, the Moscow center got control, and Yevpatoriya got the consolation prize of checking Moscow's code for errors.

As *Phobos 1* approached its destination, Moscow wanted to issue a command to turn on some of the probe's scientific equipment. Yevpatoriya's code-checking system was down, so Moscow impatiently bypassed the testing. Unfortunately, their code was missing a hyphen. The altered command accidentally activated a steering test program that shut down the probe's thrusters and caused *Phobos 1* to fall irrecoverably off course.

Although the catastrophic failure looked like the fault of one

This artist's rendering of *Phobos 1* illustrates how the probe might have examined the surface of the Martian moon if the software failures hadn't prevented it from ever reaching its destination.

careless coder, the real culprit was the software development process. Developers should have coded safeguards to ensure that a single typo couldn't possibly have mission-ending results. They also should have removed all unnecessary code before launch. Because the team had stored the steering test program in read-only memory, getting rid of it meant replacing the probe's computer entirely. To save time, developers created a software fix they (wrongly) believed would block access to the test code.

Preventable software issues also caused the loss of *Phobos 2*. Most space probes have fail-safe code to deal with emergencies. Due to time constraints, the rushed team launched *Phobos 2* without that protective code. When the probe had difficulty orienting solar panels toward the sun, the batteries drained completely before mission control could solve the problem. Cutting corners on software development saved some time and money before launch but caused the mission to fail.

SOFTWARE DEVELOPMENT LIFE CYCLE

Although few software development projects are as high stakes as space missions are, most projects are complex, time-consuming, and expensive. Because software is woven into the fabric of everyday life, bad code can have far-reaching consequences. Software issues are a main cause of recalls for life-sustaining medical devices such as pacemakers and insulin pumps. Over 15 percent of automotive recalls are software-related, with each recall costing millions of dollars. To make matters worse, the interconnectedness of the modern world means a small bug in one program can cause a cascade of problems. In 2003 electrical-grid-balancing software failed to trip an alarm when a few high-voltage power lines in Ohio shut down. Power outages rippled through eight states and parts of Canada, leaving 50 million people without power and causing $6 billion in losses.

To prevent problems, developers need to make good decisions throughout the six different stages of the software development life cycle. Only one of these six stages involves actually writing the main program. The other stages in the development cycle focus on planning, testing, and maintaining the code. Whether teams are creating accounting software or virtual reality games, they begin by gathering requirements and designing the program. After they code the program, teams focus on testing, deployment, and maintenance.

GATHERING REQUIREMENTS

Imagine a client asks for mapping software able to calculate the best possible route to various destinations. Diving into coding without more detail would end badly because "best" could mean fastest, shortest, most fuel efficient, or safest for pedestrians.

Starting in the wrong direction wastes time and money, so software development begins with establishing two types of requirements. *Functional requirements* describe what the application should do. *Nonfunctional requirements* describe how well the program should do those things—how fast, reliable, and secure it should be, and how many users it should handle at a time.

Business analysts work with clients to craft exhaustive descriptions of software requirements, written in plain language that non-developers can understand. These requirements (also called specifications or specs) often run hundreds of pages. For a mapping app, requirements might answer questions such as the following:

- » Who will use the mapping app? Delivery drivers may need to map a route with 50 stops. Ordinary drivers may just want to get from work to a new restaurant.

- » What features does the app need? Should it account for toll roads? Should it consider current traffic? Should it exclude streets too narrow for delivery trucks? Should it offer audio directions?

- » Where will the app run? Does it need to work on Windows computers, iPhones, a company's custom navigator, or on all three?

- » What are the data sources? Will maps be downloaded or accessed via satellite? Will the app need a real-time connection to information about traffic and road closures?

- » How will the user interact with the program? Does the app need to work with a touch screen or accept voice commands?

- » What level of performance is expected? Can the software take 20 seconds to calculate a route, or just two?

Because no one can keep hundreds of pages of requirements in their heads, business analysts create visual representations of program behaviors and requirements called *UML (Unified Modeling Language) activity diagrams*. These diagrams outline major software inputs, tasks, decision points, and outputs. An activity diagram for a mapping program able to calculate the fastest and shortest routes would look something like this:

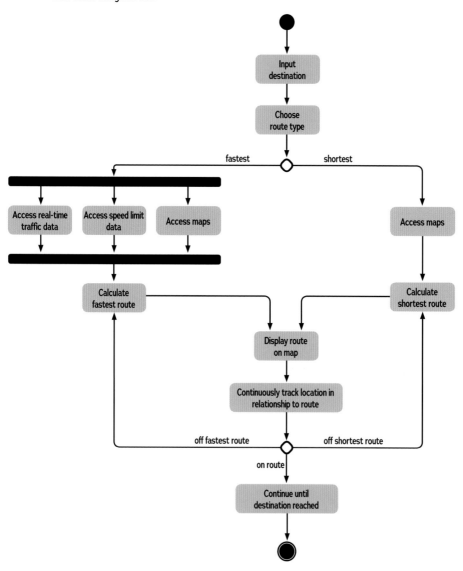

UML activity diagrams outline major software inputs, tasks, decision points, and outputs.

Software development projects often go over budget or fall behind schedule when part of the program is harder to code than developers expected. Project managers plan for problems, making sure developers will build the essential elements before tackling optional ones. To prioritize requirements, project managers typically use the MoSCoW method, which stands for **m**ust have, **s**hould have, **c**ould have, and **w**ant (or, more realistically, **w**on't have this time). An abbreviated MoSCoW list for a route-mapping program might prioritize options like this:

Must	Ability to identify shortest route, update maps, use touch screen controls
Should	Ability to choose shortest or fastest route and add multiple stops
Could	Voice commands, real-time traffic monitoring
Want	Ability to change map colors, choose different voices

ACTIVITY: SOCIAL MEDIA MUST-HAVES

Imagine you are establishing MoSCoW requirements for a new social media app. Which features would you put in the must have, should have, could have, and want categories? Consider everything from the types of devices that will run the app to how users will find friends and share content.

The real MoSCoW list for a social media app would be quite long. Here are a few options to consider:

- It must run on any brand phone, post photos and text, have a system for finding friends/following people, allow blocking, and show ads to generate profit.
- It should offer public and private accounts, work on a desktop computer, and let followers respond to posts.
- It could allow direct messages and include emojis.
- You may want it to offer photo-editing tools and allow users to post videos.

DESIGN

Software requirements tell developers what to build, but not how to build it. Giving developers only a set of requirements would be a bit like telling a construction crew to build a three-bedroom, two-bathroom house on a specific lot. A house that meets those requirements can be built in many ways. Without a detailed design telling the crew where to install support beams and run electrical lines, the crew won't be able to get started.

The same principle applies to software development. Teams of developers need blueprints explaining how to break up requirements into separate chunks of code and how those chunks of code should connect. "Some of the best programming is done on paper," explains Google developer Max Kanat-Alexander. "Putting it into the computer is just a minor detail."

Just as architects provide blueprints for construction crews, people called software architects provide coding blueprints for developers. Creating those blueprints begins with high-level design, which involves big-picture decisions about the following:

- » programming languages and coding tools
- » connections to other programs or external data sources
- » program outputs, such as reports, data files, displays, or text messages
- » security plans, including login procedures and data encryption strategies
- » whether applications should run only on the user's device or partly on a server
- » user input options, including the forms and menus that users will need
- » the order of events as data flows through the program
- » database structure, content, and location
- » program structure

The structure of a program's code depends on the programming language. A route-mapping program written in Java would have *classes* such as GPS, map, and router. Each class would have specific responsibilities, as shown in this figure. For example, the router class would be responsible for calculating the shortest and fastest routes.

GPS	Map	Router
Get latitude Get longitude	Display current location Display route	Calculate shortest route Calculate fastest route

This blueprint for a route-mapping program written in Java shows the specific responsibilities of each class.

Low-level design adds details to the high-level design, giving developers more specifics about how to write the code. For a route-mapping program, low-level design would describe how the router class will get information about the user's current location from the GPS class. It would also describe exactly how the software will combine distance, speed limits, and traffic data to find the fastest route.

CODING

Once the program design is clear, developers can finally start coding. Regardless of the design details, good code follows these same basic principles:

Write as little code as possible. Programs often perform the same tasks repeatedly. Developers could handle that by copying and pasting code, but that approach means they would have to make changes in multiple places with each update. That type of editing wastes time and leads to mistakes, so developers follow the "don't repeat yourself" (DRY) principle. Instead of writing repetitive code, developers create functions, which are like mini programs that perform a specific task. Instead of repeating code, developers just call the function each time they need it. Some developers call repetitive code WET, which stands for "write everything twice" or "waste everyone's time."

Keep code readable. Expert developer Martin Fowler wrote, "Any damn fool can write code that a computer can understand; the trick is to write code that humans can understand." Developers keep code readable by documenting the purpose of each section, keeping related elements together, following conventions for code layout, and using clear names for functions and variables. Naming a function "gelat" offers no clues to its purpose, whereas "get_latitude" makes the purpose obvious.

ACTIVITY: VACATION DESIGN

The concept of translating requirements into low-level designs applies to all projects, not just coding. To practice, design your ideal vacation, from basic requirements to a detailed low-level plan that covers all crucial elements of planning and taking the trip.

. . . .

Vacation requirements: Spend spring break on a Florida beach with my family without going into debt.

- Location
  » Research popular beaches.
  » Choose a spot.
- Travel dates
- Check school vacation days.
  » Choose travel dates.
- Lodging
  » Compare costs of various motels near the beach.
  » Book the most affordable room.
- Transportation
  » Compare costs of flying, taking a bus, or driving.
  » Choose an option balancing cost and convenience.
  » Purchase any tickets needed.
- Activities
  » Select theme park, snorkeling, swimming, and shopping opportunities.
- Payment
  » Calculate costs for travel, lodging, and activities.
  » Identify the amount to save each week, starting six months before the trip.
  » Cut weekly expenses by that amount.
- Packing
  » Clothes for each day
  » Toiletries
  » Swimsuit
  » Sandals

Most elements can be broken down further. A plan to visit a theme park, for example, might include arrival and departure time, ride order, lunch plans, and souvenir purchases.

Keeping code well organized takes active work. Between last-minute changes, contributions from multiple people, and workarounds to handle bugs, code inevitably gets messier over time. Developers call jumbled, disorganized code *a ball of mud* or *spaghetti code*. Debugging messy code makes developers miserable, because they have to spend so much time working out how pieces connect. As developer Steve McConnell wrote, "It's OK to figure out murder mysteries, but you shouldn't need to figure out code."

Write modular code. Developers don't create one monster document millions of lines long. Instead, they break programs into independent chunks, called modules. Modules are like building blocks that developers click together to make a larger whole. This approach allows many people to work on a project simultaneously. It also makes updates easy since developers only need to change the relevant module.

Save every version. Developers often rework sections of code to add features or fix problems. Often a module that worked perfectly stops working after an update to another part of the program. To minimize problems, developers keep untested code separate from finished code and save every version of the code ever written. If a change causes problems, they can simply roll back to the last working version. To manage all of those code updates, developers use *version control software* to make sure they don't accidentally overwrite someone else's work or rely on outdated code.

TESTING

Developers have a saying: "We can make software fast, cheap, or good. Pick two." Bugs are the main reason software can't be all three. The average iPhone app contains 500,000 lines of code; major programs such as Facebook have over 60 million. Simply displaying the Snapchat login screen on a computer requires 73 different web browser requests and the transfer of a megabyte of data. With so many places for things to go wrong, even the best developers write buggy code.

Although bugs are common, they can have major consequences. In 2008 London's Heathrow Airport opened a state-of-the art terminal with computerized baggage handling. The system, designed to handle 70,000 bags each day, had 132 check-in desks, 12 transfer lines, and a high-speed track for late bags. On opening day, baggage handlers repeatedly crashed the system with routine tasks, such as pulling a suitcase from the conveyer belt to get an essential item back to a passenger. The software rejected baggage handler logins and issued faulty notices about plane departures. Passengers watched confused employees steer bags away from their waiting plane. During the first 10 days of operation, software glitches stranded tens of thousands of suitcases and caused the airport to cancel over 500 flights. Trial runs with 12,000 bags had suggested the software worked, but clearly, the software needed more intensive testing.

Testing takes up a significant portion of the time and money spent on software development. To create useful, reliable software, teams do two broad types of tests. Validation tests ensure the program matches the client's requirements. Verification tests find errors in the program. In other words, validation tests make sure developers are building the right program, and verification tests make sure they are building the program right.

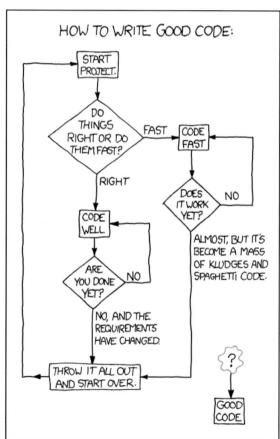

HOW TO WRITE GOOD CODE:

START PROJECT.

DO THINGS RIGHT OR DO THEM FAST? — FAST → CODE FAST

RIGHT

CODE WELL

DOES IT WORK YET? — NO → ALMOST, BUT IT'S BECOME A MASS OF KLUDGES AND SPAGHETTI CODE.

ARE YOU DONE YET? — NO

NO, AND THE REQUIREMENTS HAVE CHANGED.

THROW IT ALL OUT AND START OVER.

? → GOOD CODE

Even expert coders sometimes write "bad" code due to unanticipated needs, server loads, or other overlooked factors. When programs like the Heathrow Airport baggage handling software don't run as planned, "good" code can seem unattainable.

Verification testing is so crucial that developers often write tests before they start working on the program. Developers even write tests of tests, creating code with intentional errors to make sure their tests will catch problems. Ultimately, developers may spend as much time testing and debugging code as they do writing it. Verification tests happen at multiple levels and may include these tests:

» **Unit tests** check small segments of code. Developers write one small module, check it for errors, and rewrite it until it works as expected. Starting small makes it easier to find bugs.

» **Integration tests** explore whether two units of code work together. Code that works perfectly in isolation often breaks when combined with another component.

» **Regression tests** make sure code changes haven't created new problems. Fixing one bug often creates another, so developers rerun unit and integration tests after each change.

» **System tests** ensure every element of a program works properly. They cover user logins, program features, data storage, and security protocols. Tests may be simple, such as guaranteeing programs sort data correctly, or complex, such as feeding 10,000 fake health insurance applications into a system to look for processing errors.

» **Installation tests** verify that users actually can get programs onto their devices.

» **Compatibility tests** ensure programs run properly on different devices. Software that works perfectly on the developer's system may fail on a user's older computer.

» **Performance tests** explore the speed and reliability of programs in real-world conditions. These tests include *load testing,* which simulates a large number of people using a program simultaneously to see how quickly it gets overwhelmed.

» **Usability tests** make sure ordinary users can make sense of the program.

» **Accessibility tests** evaluate whether apps work for people with impaired vision, hearing, or mobility.

Developers usually handle unit, integration, and regression tests. Quality assurance (QA) testers often handle other aspects of testing, bombarding programs with challenges to replicate real-world use. As part of their work, they test every path a user could take through a program, including "unhappy" paths where users make strange choices. QA testers also explore every quirky situation they can think of, such as determining what happens if two users choose the same password or if a browser crashes while a user is accessing sensitive data. For the last round of testing, many companies recruit real users, called beta testers, to try out a program. Beta testers get early access to the program in exchange for their feedback.

Typical software averages 15 to 50 errors per 1,000 lines of code. Most software release with multiple bugs because tracking every problem down takes more time and money than companies can afford. Some critical software, however, goes through especially stringent testing. While writing space shuttle software, NASA developers used such scrupulous development and testing techniques that they approached zero defects per 500,000 lines of code.

DEPLOYMENT

After testing, teams deploy software, which involves much more than simply releasing apps for sale. Even with a program that works perfectly, customers need training and troubleshooting help. An understaffed or badly trained technical support team can lead to sales-tanking reviews. And, of course, newly released programs won't work perfectly. Deployment inevitably reveals undiscovered problems.

Deployment also increases demands on a company's servers—networked computers that process requests from connected devices. Servers support every interaction that goes beyond a single device, such as searching the web, checking the weather, or posting to Instagram. During deployment, each new user adds to the server load. If demand exceeds capacity, the software will run painfully slowly or crash altogether.

To reduce chaos, software development teams often spread deployment over time. There are two models for this process: staged deployments and incremental deployments. In staged deployments, they launch software to a small group of users so that they can identify and resolve issues before expanding to the next group. In incremental deployments, teams start by releasing software that only includes essential

elements. They add new features with each update, which allows them to spread bug fixes and tech support demands over time.

Even well-designed deployments can go catastrophically wrong. In 2016 Niantic Labs released *Pokémon Go*, an augmented reality game. Players walked for miles to capture Pokémon, fictional creatures that seem to physically appear in front of the player thanks to a clever blending of the virtual game with images from the phone's camera. The game drew crowds of players into the streets around the world. In New York City's Central Park, the game even caused a late-night stampede as hundreds of adults abandoned cars and shoved past one another to catch a rare Vaporeon.

Almost immediately, *Pokémon Go* had 20 million people playing each day. Or, more accurately, trying to play. The intense demand overwhelmed servers, causing the app to

CLASSIFYING BUGS

Bugs come in three main types: syntax errors, runtime exceptions, and logic errors.

Syntax errors are essentially grammatical errors. They involve misspellings, missing punctuation, or misplaced commands. They are easy to make but also easy to fix.

Runtime exceptions occur when code instructs the computer to do something it can't do. A calculation may ask the computer to divide by zero (mathematically impossible) or to divide a customer's first name by their last name (also mathematically impossible). Many runtime errors involve *infinite loops*. These occur when code tells the computer to repeat a task without directions about when to stop, leaving the computer churning endlessly. Developers can't miss runtime exceptions because they kick up error messages or crash the program.

Logic errors occur when what developers wanted the program to do isn't what they told it to do. Their code may multiply two variables they intended to add or define adults as 18-year-olds rather than as people aged 18 and over. Catching logic errors is hard because the program runs without error messages, so it seems to work but produces unexpected results.

freeze or crash and even making it impossible for players to sign in.

Before launching *Pokémon Go*, network engineers from Niantic and Google estimated demand and designed their system for a worst-case scenario of five times the expected server load. They also arranged a staged deployment, releasing the game on different days around the world so demand would ramp up slowly. Engineers thought they had everything covered, but demand wildly exceeded expectations. Players hit servers with 50 times the expected number of transactions per second.

As players fumed, Google and Niantic network engineers scrambled to make the most of limited resources. They added thousands of new servers and found ways to spread traffic across servers more efficiently. While trying to meet overwhelming demand from current players, engineers had to simultaneously redesign networks for the game's launch in Japan. One Google engineer described the process as "akin to swapping out the plane's engine in flight."

Despite persistent problems with crashes and lag even three years after the initial deployment, *Pokémon Go* remains an incredibly popular mobile game, drawing in millions of users every day from around the world.

Although problems with the *Pokémon Go* release frustrated players, it didn't cause any real harm. For hospitals, banks, military institutions, and government agencies, failed deployments can have serious consequences.

In the United Kingdom, the government's Child Support Agency was responsible for calculating child support payments, collecting money, and transferring money to custodial parents. In 2003 the agency opted to go live with new software despite unresolved bugs. Six months later, only 4 percent of custodial parents had gotten their money. Inadequately trained staff had resorted to entering fake data or deleting cases they couldn't get through the system. Three years later, employees had created 600 different workarounds for software limitations and faced a backlog of 333,000 unprocessed applications. Ultimately, the botched deployment led to $7 billion in uncollected payments.

MAINTENANCE

Because programs may stay in use for years, or even decades, developers spend more time maintaining code than writing it. On average, maintenance accounts for three-quarters of software development budgets.

Maintenance includes fixing bugs, adding features, and ensuring software works with new hardware or operating systems. A navigation app pulling map, traffic, and road closure information from external sources will need updates as those data sources change and as manufacturers release new phones. Over time, changes and additions turn once-organized programs into messy spaghetti code, so maintenance teams must refactor (organize and shorten) code to keep it reliable and easy to read.

Many maintenance fixes are minor. In 2018 Amazon's virtual assistant, Alexa, started laughing creepily at people for no apparent reason. Developers discovered Alexa was mishearing normal speech as the command, "Alexa, laugh." To keep Alexa from terrifying people, developers replaced the two-word command with the longer command, "Alexa, can you laugh?" They also programmed Alexa to say, "Sure, I can laugh," before letting out her eerie cackle.

Other maintenance issues, such as the Y2K bug, pose major challenges. In the late 1990s, many programs still drew on code from the 1960s, which stored years as two-digit numbers. This left programs with no way to distinguish between 1903 and 2003. As the year 2000 approached, this issue had the potential to create chaos. Without updates, hospital software would list a baby born on January 1, 2000, as 100 years old, since the computer would assume the year 00 meant 1900. A 100-year-old baby makes for a good story, but experts feared serious problems with airplanes, banks, utilities, and government services. Updating the world's software to handle four-digit dates took years and cost as much as $600 billion.

Testing remains crucial during the maintenance phase because updates often cause unexpected problems. Knight Capital Group, a financial service firm, released a poorly tested update in 2012, causing one of the most expensive problems in computer history. The update contained a coding error that triggered bizarre activity in the company's stock-trading program. In the hour before the company shut the program down, bad trades cost them $440 million.

STAYING AGILE

In the early days of software development, teams worked through each stage of the software development life cycle in order. They began by gathering requirements for the entire project before moving on to design, coding, testing, and release. Developers call that approach the waterfall method because the project flows from one step to the next, in order, without ever returning to previous steps.

HACKATHONS

Most software projects take months or even years. Hackathons take the complete opposite approach. These events bring people together for an extreme coding sprint, challenging teams to create an app in just a few days. Hackathons typically have an organizing theme, such as working with a particular programming language or tackling a specific problem in medicine, education, or disaster management. Organizers hope that giving people from different backgrounds a chance to have fun working together will generate creative new solutions.

The Global Game Jam, the world's largest game-creation hackathon, takes place simultaneously around the world. In 2018, 42,800 people from 108 countries participated. On the first afternoon, organizers announce a secret theme, such as deception, extinction, or ritual. Teams have just two days to create a game related to that concept. No one can create a market-ready game that fast, but many people leave with solid prototypes.

Most hackathons are friendly places, not hypercompetitive events. Many welcome beginners and help them find a team to join. The Global Game Jam even encourages non-coders to contribute ideas for games, play games to uncover bugs, or even create board games.

With thousands of hackathons offered around the world, most people

Because the waterfall method requires near-perfect specification of requirements and architecture, teams using this approach spend about 40 percent of their project time on planning. Most developers have moved away from the waterfall method because teams sometimes worked for years before discovering they'd misunderstood a requirement.

Instead, most teams use an Agile development method, cycling repeatedly through the design, building, and testing stages. Each cycle, called a sprint, tackles a small element of a project over a period of a few weeks. Agile developers often start by creating rough versions of core features and getting early client feedback. Future sprints focus on refining core features and adding new ones. This flexible approach allows developers to change course without wasting much time.

can find one close to home. Sites such as Major League Hacking (mlh.io) and Hackevents (hackevents.co) let people search for events by date, location, or theme.

Two undergraduate students collaborate on a project during hackCBS, a 24-hour hackathon that takes place each October at the Shaheed Sukhdev College of Business Studies in New Delhi, India.

Regardless of whether teams use an Agile or waterfall method, they need to pay careful attention to each aspect of the software development life cycle. Creating good software is not about sticking developers in isolated cubicles to churn out code as quickly as possible. "Measuring programming progress by lines of code is like measuring aircraft building progress by weight," goes a popular saying attributed to Microsoft founder Bill Gates. Being a great developer is less about writing brilliant code and more about taking the time to understand client requirements and communicate well with teammates.

CHAPTER 3

PROGRAMMING LANGUAGES

As a high school student in Japan, Yukihiro (Matz) Matsumoto taught himself to code. In college he worked in a programming language lab while majoring in information science. Despite his years of experience, Matz felt frustrated by programming. He wanted to concentrate on his goals for the program, "not the magical rules of the language," he explained, "I just want to say, 'print this!'"

When Matz realized the powerful, user-friendly language he wanted didn't exist, he decided to create it himself. He begin developing his own language, called Ruby, in 1993 with the goal of making programming feel fun and natural. Matz released Ruby in 1995, at the age of 28. Although Japanese was his first language, he wrote Ruby in English to make it accessible to more users. Matz also made Ruby open-source, meaning people can download Ruby for free, share it, and even modify the code used to create Ruby to make their own version.

Since that first release, Matz and his team have continued to improve and expand Ruby. Each new version releases on Christmas Day, like a brand-new toy for developers to play with. In interview after interview, Matz has said, "The goal of Ruby is to make programmers happy."

Matz seems to have succeeded. Ruby developers love the language so much that online stores sell Ruby-inspired mugs, shirts, wallets, and even boxer briefs. Developers clearly love Matz too. Amazon sells quotes from Matz on magnets, canvas prints, and engraved plaques.

Although Matz became famous for developing Ruby, he has also developed a reputation for kindness and generosity. His approach to working with others inspired the acronym MINASWAN, which stands for "Matz is nice and so we are nice." Ruby developers put MINASWAN into practice by welcoming new developers, answering questions, and encouraging mutual support so all Ruby developers learn to love coding.

RubyConf, the largest annual Ruby conference, supports MINASWAN by making the conference accessible for people with disabilities, enforcing an anti-harassment code, and providing free childcare. Yechiel Kalmenson, a rabbi-turned-developer, summarized his 2017 conference experience by writing, "I know it's already an overused trope how Rubyists are nice—it's like they're the Canadians of the programming world—but my gosh, I never met such a nice welcoming community."

SPEAKING TO COMPUTERS

Human language is ambiguous, right down to the definition of individual words. English has hundreds of words with multiple meanings. The sentence, "Miguel saw her duck," for example, can mean that Miguel just met someone's pet bird or that he just watched someone crouch down quickly. People draw on the context of a conversation to make sense of confusing language, interpreting "duck" differently depending on whether they're talking about a farm visit or an out-of-control dodgeball game.

Instead of writing code in messy, ambiguous human languages, developers use special programming languages designed for precision. That precision is necessary because computers have no common sense or awareness of context—they can only do exactly what a program tells them to do. Rod Stephens, an experienced developer, described a simple program he wrote to delete files from a single directory. Although his intent was clear, his code was not. After deleting files in the target directory, the program kept going, "cheerfully deleting every file in the system." Just five seconds of runtime did so much damage that Stephens had to reinstall his entire operating system.

ACTIVITY: COMMUNICATING CLEARLY

Giving directions clear enough for a computer to follow takes practice. To get a sense of how challenging it can be, have a friend sit out of sight with pencil and paper. Give them step-by-step directions for drawing an object, such as a pair of scissors, without telling them what they're trying to draw. Their "masterpiece" will almost certainly reveal many misunderstandings of your directions.

LOW-LEVEL LANGUAGES

At the most fundamental level, computers calculate by opening and closing electrical switches called transistors. Everything from streaming a video to guiding the path of a rocket involves nothing more than decisions about whether or not electricity should flow along a particular path.

Computer programs consist of streams of numbers, called *machine code,* that tell the computer which switches to open or close. Machine code presented in its most basic form, a stream of ones (open) and zeros (closed), is called *binary code.*

Binary code for the letters *H-E-L-L-O* reads 0100100001000101001100 0100110001001111. That string of 40 numbers isn't enough to do anything—the computer needs more code to tell it whether to store, display, or delete those letters. Developers could theoretically write programs in binary code, but it would take impossibly long and hunting for bugs would be nightmarish. Developer Charles Petzold described writing in machine code as like "eating with a toothpick."

Low-level languages are one step up from machine code but still look nothing like human language. The first developers wrote mostly in *assembly language,* a low-level language that replaces segments of ones and zeros with short words. For example, the mov command replaces the machine code that tells the computer to move information from one place to another.

Assembly code to display the words Hello, World! on an old Windows machine looks something like this:

```
org 100h
mov dx,msg
mov ah,9
int 21h
mov ah,4Ch
int 21h
msg db 'Hello, World!',0Dh,0Ah,'$'
```

That program is more human-friendly than binary code but still nowhere near intuitive. Most developers avoid low-level languages entirely, with just a few specialists using them to write programs that must be especially fast and efficient.

HIGH-LEVEL LANGUAGES

Most developers use high-level languages to write programs. Like human speech, high-level languages have units of meaning (words) arranged in a specific order (grammar). Computer grammar, or *syntax*, covers the rules for writing and punctuating statements.

Each programming language has a unique vocabulary and syntax. As with human language, details matter. "Time to eat Grandma!" means something much more ominous than "Time to eat, Grandma." Many parents could truthfully say, "I love baking, my cats, and my kids," but not many would say, "I love baking my cats and my kids."

Computers cannot run programs written in high-level languages directly, so developers use tools called *interpreters* or *compilers* to translate their programs into machine code. Developers call this process compiling their code. Different operating systems require different compilers. For an app to work on both a Mac and a Windows machine, for example, developers need to compile the code twice.

"HELLO, WORLD!"

As a tradition, one of the first tasks people tackle in a new language is displaying, "Hello, World!" on the screen. Because each language has a unique vocabulary and syntax, programs doing the exact same thing can look very different.

RUBY	PASCAL	C	JAVA

`puts "Hello, World!"`	`program hello;`
	`begin`
	`WriteLn`
	`('Hello, World!');`
	`end.`
		`int main()`
		`{`
		`  printf("Hello, World!");`
		`  return 0;`
		`}`
			`public class HelloWorld {`
			`  public static void main(String[]args) {`
			`  System.out.println("Hello, World!");`
			`  }`
			`}`

ACTIVITY: MAKING SENSE OF A PROGRAM

This program, written in Python, picks random words to complete a sentence. Running it produces sentences such as "I taunt lots of exasperated banjos because I despise them so much."

Try to match each section of the code with its purpose.

1. Fill the selected words into the sentence.
2. Create lists of verbs, nouns, adjectives, and emotions.
3. Show the sentence on-screen.
4. Choose a random verb, noun, adjective, and emotion from the word lists.
5. Access the module for choosing random items from lists.

PYTHON CODE	PURPOSE
`import random`	

`verbs = ['chase', 'critique', 'taunt', 'cuddle']`
`nouns = ['bunnies', 'banjos', 'scissors', 'umbrellas']`
`adjectives = ['fuzzy', 'combative', 'confused', 'exasperated']`
`emotions = ['adore', 'despise', 'fear', 'love']`	

`verb = random.choice (verbs)`
`noun = random.choice (nouns)`
`adjective = random.choice (adjectives)`
`emotion = random.choice (emotions)`	

`phrase = 'I ' + verb + ' lots of ' + adjective +` `    ' ' + noun + ' because I ' + emotion + ' them so much.'`	
`print(phrase)`	

To play around with the program, type it into an online Python interpreter, such as the one found at www.skulpt.org, and follow the on-screen directions to run the program. If it doesn't run, debug it by looking for typos such as misspelled words or missing parentheses. Once you get it working, try changing the word lists or the phrase they feed into.

PYTHON CODE	PURPOSE
`import random`	5

`verbs = ['chase', 'critique', 'taunt', 'cuddle']`
`nouns = ['bunnies', 'banjos', 'scissors', 'umbrellas']`
`adjectives = ['fuzzy', 'combative', 'confused', 'exasperated']`
`emotions = ['adore', 'despise', 'fear', 'love']`
	2

`verb = random.choice (verbs)`
`noun = random.choice (nouns)`
`adjective = random.choice (adjectives)`
`emotion = random.choice (emotions)`
	4

`phrase = 'I ' + verb + ' lots of ' + adjective +` `   ' ' + noun + ' because I ' + emotion + ' them so much.'`	1
`print(phrase)`	3

CHOOSING A LANGUAGE

Programmers have hundreds of languages to choose from, each with advantages and disadvantages. Some languages are designed for a specific type of device or operating system, such as Android App Inventor for Android devices. Other languages, including JavaScript and Python, are designed to work well across platforms, the combined computer and operating system used to run a piece of software. Some languages are optimized for specific tasks, such as R, which handles graphing and statistical analyses. Others, such as Java or C++, work for almost any purpose.

To use a programming language, users must download the language's software development kit and configure the programming environment to work correctly. That process can be time-consuming, so most learn-to-code websites let beginners write and run code online without downloading anything.

Developers categorize languages into four broad types—procedural, declarative, object-oriented, and functional. Each language type represents a

different programming paradigm, or way of thinking about a program's structure. Most developers learn several languages and pick whichever one is the best fit for a specific project. Typically, learning the first one takes a lot of time, because it also involves learning to think like a computer. Second and third languages come much more easily.

PROCEDURAL LANGUAGES

Procedural languages tell the computer *how* to do things. Because programs written in procedural languages run line by line from top to bottom, they are also called *top-down languages.* A procedural program to draw a square could run through a series of steps:

1. Draw a line 100 pixels long.
2. Turn 90 degrees clockwise.
3. Draw a line 100 pixels long.
4. Turn 90 degrees clockwise.
5. Draw a line 100 pixels long.
6. Turn 90 degrees clockwise.
7. Draw a line 100 pixels long.

Programs written in procedural languages have simple structures and run quickly. They are often easy for beginners to understand because they involve a logical flow of events. Low-level languages are procedural, as are most of the oldest high-level languages.

DECLARATIVE LANGUAGES

Declarative languages describe *what* should happen without specifying how. A parent who wants their teenager to clean their room could provide a list of specific chores.

1. Get the clothes on the floor into the washing machine.
2. Return dirty dishes to the kitchen.
3. Take out the trash.
4. Vacuum the carpet.

That list resembles a procedural program because it provides a set of commands to execute in order. The declarative language version would simply state, "Clean your room!" The exasperated parent doesn't care how it happens; they just want it done.

Developers often use declarative languages to configure web pages. For example, HTML code may tell a web browser to bold a section of text or display it in two columns but does not control how the browser makes that happen.

OBJECT-ORIENTED LANGUAGES

Unlike procedural languages that give step-by-step instructions, *object-oriented languages* build models that mirror the real world.

To create a virtual pet game using an object-oriented language, a developer would start by designing blueprints for broad categories, such as dogs, homes, and toys. These blueprints, called *classes*, describe all possible characteristics and behaviors related to that category. For example, the dog class would include characteristics such as dog breed, color, and name, and behaviors such as barking and playing.

Of course, a virtual pet game needs specific dogs, homes, and toys, not just blueprints for those things. Each specific instance of a dog, home, or toy is an *object*. A virtual pet game will contain many virtual dog objects, such as a chocolate lab named Rex and a white poodle named Gigi. Using object-oriented languages, developers can connect programmed objects like real-world objects, linking each virtual dog to a virtual home and a collection of virtual toys.

Well-written object-oriented programs are easy to modify, reuse, and troubleshoot. For example, if the virtual pet game won't let players name their dog, developers know the problem likely has something to do with the dog class, not the home or toy class.

FUNCTIONAL LANGUAGES

Functional programs are based on a series of expressions resembling mathematical equations. Functional code is short, predictable, and easy to debug. However, learning functional languages is tricky because it requires mastering strange concepts, such as recursive functions that refer back to themselves. Developers often use functional languages for projects requiring complex calculations, such as designing a financial fraud–detection program or creating a search engine capable of interpreting human language.

COMBINING LANGUAGES

In 2011 NASA launched the *Curiosity* rover to explore whether the Martian environment was once capable of supporting life. Along with a laser-emitting camera, an X-ray–taking robotic arm, rock grinders, water detectors, and multiple antennas, *Curiosity* also carried 3.8 million lines of code. That code, written in multiple languages, allowed *Curiosity* to communicate with Earth, monitor its own health, navigate, control high-tech equipment, and analyze samples.

Developers wrote the rover's core operational code in C because doing so allowed them to build on code written for earlier missions. NASA reuses reliable code when possible because a single bug can cause the catastrophic failure of a $100 million mission. As Gerard Holzmann, head of NASA's JPL Laboratory for Reliable Software, said, "Better the devil you know . . ."

Developers used two general-purpose languages, C++ and Java, to write *Curiosity*'s Robot Sequencing and Visualization Program. The million lines of code

The *Curiosity* rover takes a selfie on the surface of Mars. Its developers worked tirelessly for it to be able to do this.

in the program control the rover's robotic arm and allow it to drive across the surface of Mars. Each day, mission control transmits movement-related commands to *Curiosity*. Developers write those commands in XML and then translate them into binary code.

Curiosity's developers used Python to write code tests and custom software called Scrub to track errors and bug fixes. It took a team of 40 developers about five years to create *Curiosity*'s code. Because the code needed to be perfect, the entire

POPULAR PROGRAMMING LANGUAGES

LANGUAGE	PRIMARY PARADIGM	DESCRIPTION
C	Procedural	One of the first high-level languages. Used for embedded firmware and applications closely tied to operating systems.
C++	Object-oriented	A versatile, enhanced version of C used for everything from game development to business software.
C#	Object-oriented	Microsoft's alternative to Java. Used for web apps, game development, and Microsoft apps. (Pronounced "C sharp," not "C hashtag.")
HTML	Declarative	An easy-to-read language used to control text presentation on websites.
Java	Object-oriented	A general purpose language, portable across platforms. Used for desktop, web, and mobile apps and taught in Advanced Placement classes.
JavaScript	Multi paradigm	Used for interactive features on web pages, such as uploading pictures or moving an email to a new folder. Unrelated to Java, despite the similar name.

team produced only 10 lines of fully tested code per hour.

Their work did not end with the rover's launch: *Curiosity*'s code changes constantly. In 2013, when sharp rocks and dust began to take a toll on *Curiosity*, NASA developers uploaded a wheel-protecting traction-control program. In 2015 they uploaded artificial intelligence software so *Curiosity* can independently identify rocks worth testing. The program allows *Curiosity* to keep working even when the rotation of Mars places it outside NASA's transmission range.

LANGUAGE	PRIMARY PARADIGM	DESCRIPTION
PHP	Procedural	Powerful, compatible across platforms, and easy to learn. Used for websites with frequently changing content, such as Facebook.
Python	Object-oriented	General purpose and easy to learn. Used for data analysis, scientific applications, games, robotics, apps, and web development.
R	Functional	Used to conduct statistical analyses and display results.
Ruby	Object-oriented	Easy to learn, often used for web apps. Linked to development tools such as Ruby on Rails, which speed up development by simplifying repetitive tasks.
SQL	Declarative	Used to search and update databases. Often used in combination with other languages.
Swift	Object-oriented	Developed by Apple, often used to write apps for iPhones, iPads, Apple Watches, and Macs.

BUILDING BLOCKS

Despite differences in vocabulary and syntax, programming languages share core building blocks. Every language offers a way to define variables, repeat behaviors, and control how the program responds to events.

Variables define information the program needs to store or interact with. Variables may represent simple data, such as text or numbers, or complex data structures, such as an online shopping cart. In a social media app, variables might store information such as this:

```
firstName = "Marco"
currentAge = 16
profilePublic = false
friends = {"Celia", "Mallory", "Jiro", "Ibrahim" . . . }
```

Loops allow programs to repeat a behavior. Programmers could tell a computer to draw a square by listing steps for each line individually: draw a line, turn 90 degrees, draw a line, turn 90 degrees, and so on. That approach works but is inefficient. Loops simplify those commands to this:

```
Repeat 4 times: (Draw a line 100 pixels long. Turn 90
degrees clockwise.)
```

This so-bad-it's-good joke illustrates the challenge of loops: "Why did the developer get stuck in the shower? Because the shampoo directions said, 'Lather, rinse, repeat.'" When developers use loops, they need to tell the computer when to stop repeating an action. Otherwise, they create an infinite loop, which churns through the same task endlessly until someone forces the program to close.

To prevent lifelong shampooing, developers could use a rinse-counting variable to control the loop. The rinse-counting variable would start at zero and go up by one after each rinse. The shampooing loop would end when `rinse = 2`.

Conditional statements, or if-then statements, allow developers to control how computers respond to events. If-then commands are common in real life. Parents of preschoolers say, "IF you eat your vegetables, THEN you can have dessert."

Bosses say, "IF you meet the sales target, THEN you get a bonus."

Conditional statements often include an "else" statement to describe an alternative path. For example, in a virtual pet game, the pet selection process would look something like this:

```
Display pet selection menu.
IF player clicks dogs, THEN display dog breed selection menu.
ELSE display cat breed selection menu.
```

Most programs depend on a large number of conditional statements to control the flow of events. Developers can use flowcharts to represent how those events will unfold.

ACTIVITY: DECISION-MAKING FLOWCHARTS

To get a sense of how conditional statements control the flow of a program, create a decision-making flowchart on any topic you like, based on the example below. Your chart could cover decisions about lending money to friends, choosing a pet, or accepting a follow request on social media from your grandma.

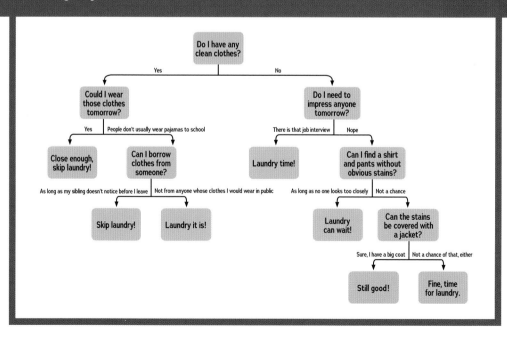

Functions are essentially mini programs that provide directions for a specific task. Developers write code to define a function and then call that function by name within the main program whenever they want to repeat the task.

For example, a virtual pet game may allow players to own multiple pets. With each adoption, the game may prompt players to name their pet and buy new toys. The game may also trigger existing pets to display jealousy. Rather than writing that code separately for dogs and cats or for second pets and fourth pets, the developer could create a reusable function called `adopt` that includes all those actions.

Besides writing their own functions, developers also have access to code libraries containing commonly used functions. Developers rarely write code to sort lists or generate random numbers—they simply call the function they need from the library.

ACTIVITY: LOOKING FOR PATTERNS

Identifying patterns allows developers to write better code. Imagine trying to represent the melody and lyrics of your favorite song. What patterns would make it possible for a computer program to re-create the song without having to store every note and word individually?

Turn to page 124 for the answer.

USING DEVELOPMENT TOOLS

At first glance, computer programs can look like a jumble of symbols and strange words. Fear of memorizing so many unfamiliar things can scare people away before they give coding a try. But even experienced developers haven't memorized all the function names and syntax rules—they rely on development tools to handle the details.

Developers typically work in **integrated development environments (IDEs)** that put crucial tools in one place. Every IDE has a code editor with drop-down menus to help developers choose commands. As developers type, the code editor offers suggestions for the next step and displays options associated with each command. It also handles syntax, catches typos, highlights missing pieces, and links to sample code. Using these tools, developers can focus on ideas rather than trying to figure out where to add a semicolon. IDEs usually also include debuggers and version control tools to keep track of old code.

JULIA LIUSON, DEVELOPING FOR DEVELOPERS

Almost a quarter of developers use Visual Studio, the world's most popular IDE. With Visual Studio, developers can examine the structure of a program, test and debug code, collaborate with others, and fix disorganized code. The program even auto-completes code and highlights coding errors, similar to the way word processors use squiggly red lines to reveal misspelled words.

Software developer Julia Liuson has been central to the design of Visual Studio since Microsoft released the first version in 1997. She has progressed from entry-level developer to team lead to manager to corporate vice president for Visual Studio at Microsoft. Liuson oversees everything related to Visual Studio, from designing the user interface to improving integrated testing tools.

Liuson came to the United States from China to study electrical engineering at the University of Washington. When she began working at Microsoft in 1992, she was the only woman on a floor with 100 employees. After meetings in other buildings, she would discover toilet seats in the woman's bathroom still up from a cleaning the night before—not a single woman had used the bathroom all day.

Unsurprisingly, Liuson initially felt intimidated at Microsoft. She recalled feeling stressed about a team member who often used words she couldn't understand. Initially, she blamed herself, thinking, "My vocabulary is not that good, I just don't know what he's talking about." Eventually, she began to suspect her American colleagues didn't understand him either. "It was a good lesson of courage," Liuson said, "because at some point I just looked at him and said English is not my first language, tell me, what does that word actually mean?" As soon as she asked, other people piped up to admit they didn't know the word either.

In her early years, Liuson avoided programs intended to support women in tech, because she wanted to be seen as a software developer, not specifically a female software developer. As a vice president, Liuson sees creating a diverse and inclusive culture as one of her core responsibilities. So she supports developers by creating both great programming tools and great work environments.

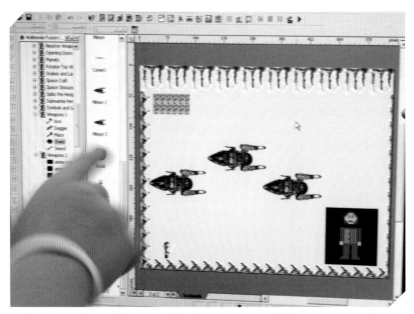

Ian Bergman, 10, shows off his game, "Splee Chase thru Time," which he created at a coding camp designed for kids at the University of California, Irvine.

Software development kits are collections of free, downloadable resources linked to a specific programming language or hardware platform. These kits usually come with tutorials, sample code, libraries of prewritten code, and IDEs. Companies provide them to encourage developers to use their language or develop for their platform. For example, the Android kit makes it easy for programmers to turn Java code into apps for Android phones.

Game engines make it easier to create video games. All games, from flight simulators to role-playing fantasy games, need to accept user input, display graphics, animate characters, and detect collisions. Smoke should rise and dropped objects should fall, but re-creating gravity in the game world requires an advanced understanding of physics that few developers have. Game engines take care of the math for developers, allowing them to replicate Earth's gravity or simulate outer space. They also help developers handle animation, sound effects, online play, menus, and game levels. Even major video game developers use free game engines such as Unity and Unreal to build their games.

Application-programming interfaces (APIs) work like adaptors. They connect two pieces of software, even if the programs were written in different languages by unrelated companies. People use an API each time they copy and paste between programs or post to Instagram from their phone's camera roll. At a Girls Who Code program, one group used a Weather Underground API to create a hairstyle suggestion app. After users enter their zip code, the program snags the local forecast and suggests frizz-free styles for wet and humid days.

APIs allow apps created by independent developers to communicate with popular programs such as Snapchat, Twitter, or Instagram. For example, with Snapchat APIs, developers can write apps that allow users to sign in with their Snapchat credentials, import their Bitmoji, or share images to their Snapchat story.

Together, these tools make it easy for developers to translate their ideas into a language computers can understand. They free developers to focus on their creative goals, rather than low-level details, and make it easier for new programmers to dive in.

CHAPTER 4
MANAGING AND MANIPULATING DATA

As a *Star Wars* fan growing up in Syria, Dina Katabi was intrigued by the idea of the Force, an energy connecting everything in the universe. "I would be sitting at home," she said, "just concentrating and focusing, trying to feel the Force." Despite her efforts, Katabi never did feel it. But now, as a professor at MIT, she uses radio waves to create her own version of the Force.

Radio waves travel through the air, like ripples through water. When these invisible waves collide with people or objects, they bounce back as reflections. Katabi realized she could use those reflections to perceive things she couldn't see directly. Detecting radio waves was easy—the challenge lay in making sense of the radio wave data her sensors collected.

Radio waves don't reflect just once, explains Katabi. "You get very complex reflections where the same signal reflects off me and then off you, and then off the ceiling, then off the floor. And you have to make sense of that mess." She and

Dina Katabi (*left*) speaks with FCC chair Julius Genachowski (*middle*) and MIT professor Hari Balakrishnan in 2013.

her team developed a program able to disentangle the chaotic jumble of data from the reflected signals. Just as bats and dolphins use sonar signals to "see," Katabi captures movement with the help of a device that emits radio waves and detects the reflections.

"Radio signals are amazing creatures," she says. "If you know how to manipulate them, they can capture very minute motions." Katabi clearly knows how. Her software can detect a person's position, movement, heart rate, breathing, and sleep stage. Not only does her device work in the dark, like X-ray vision, it can use the data it collects to see through walls.

Katabi built her system to help the millions of older adults who need emergency treatment for falls each year. When her software detects a fall, it texts a caregiver or calls an ambulance. Her system also tracks changes in breathing, activity level, heart rate, or sleep patterns over time. For people with heart or lung disease, catching those changes early gives doctors time to intervene before problems get serious.

To turn radio waves into a detailed picture of a person's movements, Katabi's program needs to handle a huge amount of data. That challenge isn't unique to her software, however. Developers define data as any information processed or stored by a computer. No matter what a program does, or how complex that program is, all programs have the same core function of managing and manipulating data.

DATA EVERYWHERE

Some of the data central to programs is relatively obvious. Online shopping programs need data about items for sale, such as the price and number of items in stock. Health insurance software needs data about the medical services patients have received and the cost of those services. Video streaming apps decode a flood of compressed data, convert it into information about the color and location of pixels, and display the transformed data on a screen. Katabi's device pulls in radio wave data and translates it into information about movement.

Programs also collect (or create) some surprising data. Retail software may collect data about every item a shopper views, when they searched, and whether they opened the last sales promo email. Health insurance software logs the source of each request for patient information and documents every exchange of data with doctors or hospitals. Having that information helps the company identify unauthorized attempts to access a patient's private medical information.

ACTIVITY: ADVANCED WEB SEARCHES

Almost 60 percent of web searches include only one or two words. Although that works for simple cases, an overly broad search can lead a musician shopping for a new bass to some wildly off-topic bass fishing websites. With advanced search techniques, people can filter out unwanted results.

Play around with the search strategies shown below to see how they influence results. You could search anything from your favorite celebrity to cake recipes. (Or put them together—searching "Beyoncé cake recipe" leads to a recipe for Beyoncé's daughter's six-layer birthday cake.)

TECHNIQUE	EXAMPLE	RESULT
Use more keywords.	Search "electric bass reviews" instead of "bass."	Searching "bass" produces 880 million results. Searching "electric bass reviews" drops that to 109 million.
Put a minus sign in front of unwanted words.	bass -fish	This returns sites that include the word "bass" but not the word "fish."
Use quotations marks to get an exact match for a string of words.	"used electric bass"	This returns only websites that have the words "used electric bass" in that order.
Combine searches by putting "OR" between them.	"used electric bass" OR "used electric guitar"	This returns websites with information about used electric guitars or basses.
Add a * as a placeholder for missing words.	"used * bass"	This returns websites with terms such as, "used upright bass" or "used vintage bass."

BE NORMAL

Software design goes hand in hand with data management, even for fun apps and games. Multiplayer games like *Fortnite*, *League of Legends*, and *World of Warcraft* need to store information covering the following:

- » each player's login dates and times
- » changes in character level, ability, health, and resources over time
- » details of current and past alliances
- » the start point, end point, path, and duration of every movement
- » the location and duration of every interaction with another character or object

Fortnite had 125 million players in 2018, which translates to a lot of data. Basic data management tools, such as spreadsheets, don't have the speed or capacity to handle that much data. When developers set up databases incorrectly, their programs become painfully slow or take up too much storage space.

Companies such as Amazon, which have hundreds of millions of customers, take collecting and storing information seriously. Amazon tracks virtually every customer behavior: searches, items viewed, items purchased, time spent considering each item, payment methods, shipping decisions, returns, reviews, and even every word highlighted in a Kindle book.

Amazon could arrange all of that data in one massive spreadsheet, adding a new line to the table for each item a customer views. This sample table shows just a few of the columns a spreadsheet would need to track customer behavior. The real spreadsheet would need thousands of columns and would be trillions of lines long.

First Name	Last Name	Birthdate	Address	Phone	Date	Item ID	Time Viewed	Qty.	Payment Method
Jane	Doe	07/01/2011	123 Oak St.	123-456-7890	10/23/19	125730	12:30 p.m.	1	Visa ending in 1234
Jane	Doe	07/01/2011	123 Oak St.	123-456-7890	10/23/19	257103	12:32 p.m.	4	Visa ending in 1234
Jane	Doe	07/01/2011	123 Oak St.	123-456-7890	10/24/19	967234	12:40 p.m.	0	
Juan	Garcia	01/01/1972	321 Elm Rd.	987-654-3210	11/04/18	190375	7:14 a.m.	1	Gift card 5678
Juan	Garcia	01/01/1972	321 Elm Rd.	987-654-3210	11/04/18	089264	7:17 a.m.	3	Gift card 5678
Juan	Garcia	01/01/1972	321 Elm Rd.	987-654-3210	11/04/18	375103	7:23 a.m.	1	Visa ending in 9999

Over the years, an Amazon customer may view thousands of items. Listing their name, address, and phone number on each of those thousands of rows would waste a lot of storage space. Repeating that information also makes updates and corrections difficult. What if Jane Doe was born in 2001 but accidentally entered 2011 when she made her first purchase? If Amazon stored all of its data in one giant spreadsheet, it would have to correct her birthdate in a separate row for every item she had ever viewed. That correction would be time-consuming and could easily miss some of the thousands of times the wrong date appeared. Amazon would end up with an enormous, mistake-filled spreadsheet.

To prevent that problem, developers design databases to avoid repeated information. Instead of creating one giant spreadsheet, they create several separate tables, such as a customer table, an order table, and a shipment table. Jane Doe's identifying information would only be stored once, in a single row in the customer table, so correcting her birthdate would only require one change. Databases that minimize repeated information are called normalized databases. They are more complicated than a single spreadsheet but require less storage space and make updates easy.

To visualize relationships between tables, developers draw diagrams. In these diagrams, boxes represent tables and include a list of all the variables within that table. Lines connecting boxes show the relationship between tables.

This simplified diagram shows the basic structure of a normalized sales database. Details about items for sale go in the item table and details about customers go in the customer table. Information about items ordered belongs in the order content table, which connects to the order table. The order table holds information unique to that order, such as the order date, and connects to shipment and payment tables.

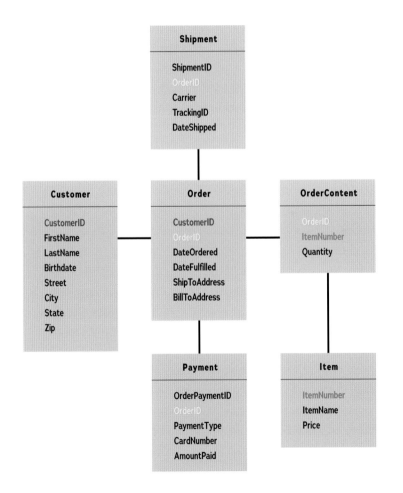

Developers use shared identifying variables to link tables. In this example, the customer ID variable connects names and addresses from the customer table to purchases stored in the order table.

Because tables are linked, companies can use database queries to create reports on any combination of data. They can explore differences in the types of items teenagers and adults buy, identify which items people often buy together, or track average shipment times by state.

HOW ALGORITHMS SOLVE PROBLEMS

Although managing data is essential, it only gets you so far. Programs need to use that information to solve problems or accomplish tasks. For that, developers need *algorithms*—ordered, step-by-step directions telling a program what to do. Algorithms are not new or unique to computers. Any set of directions carried out in order counts. One of the oldest written algorithms is a 4,000-year-old clay tablet describing the steps in long division. Cookie recipes are dessert-making algorithms. Driving directions are path-finding algorithms.

Most programs weave together many separate algorithms. Some solve simple problems, such as sorting email messages by arrival time. Others solve complex problems, such as determining which emails contain important content.

Many algorithms, such as the route-finding algorithms used by UPS, allow people to tackle problems that would be unsolvable without the speed and power of computers. Worldwide, UPS drivers deliver over 20 million packages each day, with individual drivers averaging 120 stops. Planning an efficient route could take days because the number of possible paths is astronomical. For 10 stops, the number of possible routes is $10 \times 9 \times 8 \times 7 \times 6 \times 5 \times 4 \times 3 \times 2 \times 1$, or 3,628,800 potential paths. For 120 routes, the number of possible paths "far exceeds the age of the earth in nanoseconds," says Jack Levis, UPS director of process management. Even a computer can't calculate all the possible paths, so UPS spent four years developing a route-mapping algorithm capable of quickly finding a reasonable path. Compared to its old software, the new program shaved 100 million miles (160 million km) off delivery routes and saved UPS about $400 million each year.

WHAT'S IN A WORD?

The data stored by word-processing programs goes far beyond the text shown on the screen. In fact, the .docx "file" that stores a Microsoft Word document is actually a zipped container holding many folders and files. To look inside, change the .docx part of a document's name to .zip and then right-click to unzip the resulting folder. (If you try this, use a copy of your file, not the original!).

An unzipped Word document has a folder called _rels, which holds data detailing the relationship between .docx files. The docProps folder holds files describing every person who has worked on the document and when they made changes. Plagiarism checkers use this hidden information to ensure students did their own work. Forensic scientists use it to look for secretly altered files. Other folders store information about fonts, layouts, spelling and grammar errors, images, and previous versions. The file called document.xml contains the text of the document plus formatting directions. XML is a markup language used to control the display of text. You can look at .xml files using a text editor, such as Notepad.

Displayed on this screen is an example of XML markup language. Many software development tools automatically apply colors to make it easier for developers to read and differentiate elements of code.

Turn to page 124 for the answer.

A NEED FOR SPEED

Given that scientists have catalogued almost one million animal species, trying to guess which animal a person is thinking of during a guessing game could take a long time. You could make some educated guesses, such as guessing elephant before axolotl, but it would still be a daunting task. The 20 questions game, which allows people to ask yes or no questions, makes guessing much easier.

The questions people ask while trying to guess an animal resemble an animal identification algorithm. Experienced players can often identify an animal correctly with just a few questions. That is because they ask questions that rule out large numbers of animals, such as "Is it a mammal?" or "Does it live on land?" Young children often take longer because they ask inefficient questions, such as "Is it green?"

So, not all algorithms work equally well. Badly chosen questions beat random guessing, but both are less effective than well-chosen questions. Inefficient algorithms don't matter if people are killing time playing 20 questions, but they make computer programs annoyingly slow.

Often algorithms that make intuitive sense are unworkable with large data sets. Imagine trying to sort a pile of books alphabetically by the author's last name. For each book, you could scan the shelf from left to right, inserting the book when you reach the right location. Sorting each book requires one pass through the shelf. On average, you would have to scan through half the books each time to find the correct spot. That works for a small collection, but Amazon lists almost 50 million books. To digitally sort that catalog by author name, the program would have to make 50 million passes through the data, scanning an average of 25 million books per pass.

Developers solved that problem with the less intuitive but more efficient merge sort algorithm. To sort by name, this algorithm chooses pairs of random names and

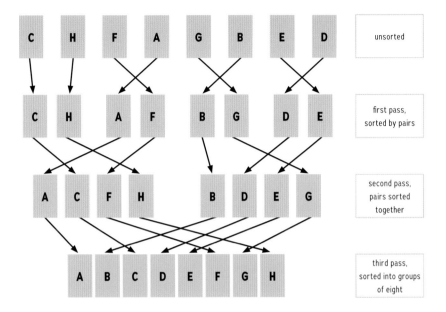

| | | | | | | | | unsorted |
| C | H | F | A | G | B | E | D | |

| | | | | | | | first pass, sorted by pairs |
| C | H | A | F | B | G | D | E | |

| | | | | | | | second pass, pairs sorted together |
| A | C | F | H | B | D | E | G | |

| | | | | | | | third pass, sorted into groups of eight |
| A | B | C | D | E | F | G | H | |

alphabetizes within those pairs. Next, it alphabetizes two sets of sorted pairs at a time, producing alphabetized groups of four. At each stage, the algorithm sorts two sets together at a time. Three passes through the data produces alphabetized groups of eight, and four passes produces groups of 16. With this method, Amazon could sort its book catalog with 26 passes rather than 50 million.

ACTIVITY: 20 QUESTIONS, ANIMAL EDITION

Have a friend try to guess which animal you are thinking of by asking yes or no questions. Map the path their questions take. If you can, play the game with some young children. How does their approach to the animal identification problem differ? Which approaches seem most successful?

Then design your own animal identification algorithm. Choose a starting question. From there, decide which question would be triggered by a "yes" or "no" response to that question. Keep going until you have created a flowchart showing the branching series of questions you could use to identify an animal as quickly as possible.

Turn to page 125 for the answer.

ALGORITHMS EVERYWHERE

Algorithms shape almost everything that happens online, from the ads people see to the results of their web search. Because good sales algorithms translate to great profits, companies guard their marketing and pricing algorithms as trade secrets.

Retailers feed customer data into algorithms to optimize advertisements, tailor sales offers, and customize pricing. Algorithms created for stores such as Target use customers' purchase history to prepare individualized coupon packs. Amazon's algorithms use customers' search histories, past purchases, wish lists, location, and product reviews to determine which items to display. Customers whose zip codes and purchase histories suggest wealth will see high-end products. Bargain hunters and customers living in low-income communities will see products that are more basic.

Pricing algorithms help retailers sell their products at the highest possible price. Airfare pricing algorithms change fares based on the day of the week, time of day, and customer's zip code. Orbitz, a travel-planning site, shows higher prices to people doing their travel planning on an expensive computer. Ride-sharing apps such as Uber and Lyft use surge-pricing algorithms to increase fares as demand spikes, meaning that riders pay more on rainy days and after concerts. Online, dynamic-pricing algorithms automatically raise prices on top-selling items or during popular shopping times.

Badly designed pricing algorithms can cause strange problems. In one case, competing booksellers were using algorithms to adjust their prices relative to each other. One seller updated prices daily to fall just above the other seller's price. The second seller was also resetting prices daily based on the first seller's price. Since algorithms lack common sense and simply do what they're programmed to do, both sellers' prices spiraled upward, ultimately driving the price of a $35 book to $23,698,655.93. Unsurprisingly, neither retailer made a sale at that price.

Although retailers design algorithms to wring more money from consumers, customers can also manipulate algorithms to work in their favor. Leaving items overnight in an online shopping cart may trigger a price drop. Late night shopping can mean better prices—fewer people shop at that time so algorithms drop prices to tempt more people into buying.

Algorithms also determine the results of web searches. Search algorithms are complex formulas that rank pages based on hundreds of factors, including these:

>> how often search terms appear on the page

>> how many reputable sites link to the page

>> the website's publication date

>> adherence to security protocols

>> how often others have visited the page

Search algorithms also include factors unique to each person, such as websites they've visited, their current location, and whether they're searching on a phone and need a mobile-friendly site. Searching "pizza" produces different search results (and advertisements) for a New Yorker who orders takeout every night and a Nebraskan who regularly reads cooking blogs. Search algorithms incorporate recent trends into search results, prioritizing breaking news about a bank robbery over older stories.

Because most people enter only a few words per search, search engines must predict what people want based on limited information. Natural-language algorithms help determine whether "bank" means a place to put money or a riverside picnic spot.

Predictive algorithms make searching easier by offering auto-complete suggestions based on common searches, an individual's search history, and their current location. Google estimates its predictive search function saves humanity a collective 200 years' worth of typing every day.

SEARCH ENGINES ARE INDEX ENGINES

Search engine is a slightly deceptive term because typing keywords into the Google or Bing search box doesn't actually launch a search of the over 1.8 billion websites in the world. Google alone gets 40,000 search requests per second. Their search engine would be far too slow if each query triggered a hunt through all of the internet's data to see which web pages might be relevant.

Instead, search engines manage an internet's worth of data by indexing sites in advance. Just as a book's index makes it easy for readers to find information, Google's index makes it easy for its search engine to return useful results. Google's index includes "an entry for every word seen on every web page." Besides indexing sites, search engines also speed results by preparing responses in advance for most searches. Top searches in 2017 included slime recipes, the "cash me outside" meme, Hurricane Irma, and "Despacito." When people searched those topics, search engines had presorted lists of useful websites ready to go.

SPAM-FIGHTING ALGORITHMS

In 2018 *spam* (unwanted messages sent in bulk) made up almost half of all emails sent, a whopping 14 billion unwanted messages each day. Without spam-filtering algorithms, offers for dodgy pharmaceuticals and get-rich-quick schemes would flood inboxes. At best, weeding through the junk would be an annoying waste of time. At worst, it would put vulnerable people at the mercy of con artists.

Spam filters can easily block messages that come from blacklisted email accounts or link to blacklisted websites. Unfortunately, that approach doesn't go very far—spammers just open new email accounts and set up new websites.

To outsmart spammers, developers have created algorithms that score emails on hundreds of elements and send high-scoring messages straight to the spam folder. These anti-spam algorithms flag the following:

- phrases unlikely to turn up in legitimate emails, such as "Nigerian prince" or "Rake in Ca$h now!!!!"
- strange spacing designed to sneak messages through spam filters by replacing, "Buy now!" with "B U Y N O W !"
- emails riddled with exclamation points, dollar signs, bright fonts, or flashing text
- signs of deception, such as links to Amaz0n.com
- emails containing only images (often an attempt to sneak spam past text filters)
- messages sent to an unreasonable number of people
- messages most recipients delete without opening

No filter works perfectly—some spam slips through and some legitimate messages get flagged—so developers design spam filters to learn from mistakes. When users report spam that reached their inbox or pull a message from the spam folder, those behaviors shape how the algorithm handles similar messages in the future.

Building on that success, Google has expanded its use of predictive algorithms with the Smart Reply feature, which scans the text of emails and suggests responses. For an email containing a dinner invitation, Smart Reply might offer options such as "Sounds great!" or "Sorry, I can't make it." The algorithms learn from each individual's responses, so over time, suggested responses reflect a person's tendency to use exclamation points or say "Brilliant!" instead of "Great!" Designing the feature was tricky because the options suggested have no meaning to the algorithm. In the prototyping stage, Smart Reply kept suggesting "I love you" and "Sent from my iPhone" as options—neither of which are great responses to business correspondence.

Describing the work developers do as "coding" implies that they spend their time focusing on the low-level details of programming languages. In reality, developers spend most of their time thinking about higher-level concepts, such as managing data and designing algorithms. Coding is a creative endeavor, not a rote activity.

ACTIVITY: PREDICTIVE TEXT

Texting apps use predictive algorithms to complete words and offer suggestions for the next word. Because these algorithms draw on past messages, each person gets different suggestions. Predictive text games illustrate how this works.

Start a text to a friend, using one of the prompts below. From there, choose one of your texting app's suggested options. Try the same prompt several times to see how your initial choice shapes the outcome. Have someone else try the same prompt on their own phone. How did the differences between you lead to differences in the messages you created?

Here are starting prompts:

I hid the money in the . . .

Long ago in a galaxy . . .

My lawyer told me not to . . .

Here are two sample predictive text outcomes.

Parent's phone:

> Long ago in a galaxy of carpooling to practice the tennis match was a great time with the kids.

Teen's phone:

> Long ago in a galaxy that was not a bad place for me the most important part was that I was going out of school.

CHAPTER 5
THE PSYCHOLOGY OF SOFTWARE

Software developers spend years learning how to break problems into the smallest possible components and chain solutions together with perfect logic. Although this approach produces the best possible set of directions for computers, developers must also consider the needs of computer users. Unlike computers, people are often illogical, confused, and error-prone. When developers fail to consider the human side of the equation, their programs may frustrate or even harm people.

Tristan Harris, Google's former design ethicist, has devoted his life to understanding how software affects people. When Harris trained as a magician, he manipulated people's attentional blind spots to pull off illusions. "Once you know how to push people's buttons," he explains, "you can play them like a piano." Now, as a self-described "expert on how technology hijacks our psychological vulnerabilities," he focuses on how addictive software does just that.

Smartphones exert a gravitational pull, with some sources reporting that the average person checks their phone 150 times a day. Many people automatically

Tristan Harris compares apps' functionality to that of slot machines. By constantly checking to see if you have new notifications on Facebook or photos to look at on your Instagram feed, you are playing a form of a slot machine. Sometimes you get big rewards, but mostly you end up wasting time.

reach for their phone with each new-message chime, ignoring people in the room in favor of coupon offers and snaps from random acquaintances. A quick glance often leads to an unplanned hour scrolling through posts. Harris believes those choices are caused by addictive software rather than reflecting people's true priorities.

The greatest risk of addiction comes from situations that offer occasional rewards at unknown times. When gamblers play slot machines, they keep pulling the lever because they know the payout will come eventually as long as they keep playing. With smartphones, each glance is like pulling the slot machine lever. Usually nothing exciting happens, but sometimes you get a snap from your crush or discover your Instagram post got tons of likes.

App makers take advantage of that addictive potential, designing notifications to alert users to every minor event. "It's as if all of our technology is basically only asking our lizard brain what's the best way to just impulsively get you to do the next tiniest thing with your time," says Harris. Apps become junk food—delicious and hard to resist but ultimately unhealthy.

The relentless pull of smartphones has real costs. Psychologists tested the focus of over 500 college students who put their smartphones on silent mode and placed them facedown on their desks, in their bags, or outside the classroom. Students randomly assigned to put their phone outside scored higher on memory tests than those who could see their phone. Students didn't recognize that their silenced, facedown phone impaired their concentration, but the brain drain was clear.

Harris wants developers to turn attention-manipulating tools on their heads, helping people to focus on their goals instead of their screens. To help developers make that shift, Harris cofounded the Center for Humane Technology, which suggests addiction-reducing features such as these:

- » setting notifications to arrive in batches at user-selected times

- » notifying people when they spend more time on an app than they intended

- » delaying the arrival of nonurgent messages when people are working or with friends

- » displaying the number of times an app has been opened that day

- » writing algorithms that prioritize real news over clickbait

ADDICTIVE APPS

In theory, developers create software to benefit people. In practice, many people seem to be working for their apps. Often that addiction happens by design. Companies such as YouTube, Facebook, Snapchat, and Instagram make money by showing ads and selling user data. The more time people spend on the app, the more money companies make. Users think they are getting a free product. In reality, they are the product, with app developers profiting by selling their attention.

To maximize profits, Facebook continually tweaks algorithms for the ads and posts they show each user, refining them to display content that produces the most ad clicks. Streaming video apps such as YouTube and Netflix keep people online by autoplaying the next video. This clever approach means it takes more work to quit watching than to keep going. People who meant to study or go to bed end up tempted into just one more video.

For social media apps, psychology research informs the design of everything from sign-up procedures to displays of follower counts. Snapchat invented streaks, a count of how many days in a row people have sent snaps to one another, to make sure people would open the app daily. Some kids feel so driven to maintain streaks that they have friends manage their account when they're away from their phone. Many start their day by blasting messages to hundreds of people, even when it feels like a stressful obligation.

While many consider it antisocial to always be on your phone, it is also true that social media, texting, and the internet allow people to connect and socialize in new, seemingly infinite ways. The social and psychological effects of this constant connection are a hot subject of scientific research.

Social media apps also take advantage of the psychological need for connection and approval. Constant notifications trigger people's fear of missing out—ignoring a chime might leave you out of the loop. Read indicators, such as Snapchat's red outline, tell people when their message has been seen. This creates pressure for recipients to respond immediately because "leaving someone on read" is rude.

Adults struggle with that sense of obligation too. LinkedIn, a career-networking site, notifies people of each invitation to connect. When they accept a connection, LinkedIn encourages them to send connection requests of their own. Those requests launch another round of notifications, luring in waves of people who never intended to visit LinkedIn that day.

MONEY MATTERS

The original profit model, or way of making money, for software was simple: developers sold software directly to customers. Many companies still follow that approach, selling mobile apps to smartphone users for a few bucks or business software to large corporations for millions.

More complex profit models draw on human psychology to make money. In the *freemium model,* companies give away a free basic version, hoping to lure customers into buying the premium version. Dropbox offers free online storage, Skype offers free video calls, and Spotify offers free streaming music. Upgrading to paid accounts gives users more space, more powerful features, or fewer ads. Sales pitches encouraging customers to upgrade often take advantage of people's tendency to feel guilty about taking something without giving anything back. They remind people of the benefits they've gotten from the program and ask them to support developers in return. Even when customers don't upgrade, the company still benefits because having lots of free users helps generate buzz. Some freemium products offer upgrades in exchange for promoting the app on social media.

Other profit models take advantage of people's tendency to impulsively spend small amounts of money without much thought. Many free games sell clues or extra lives for a dollar at the moment people most want them. These microtransactions hardly feel like spending money, especially because they typically draw from an already-approved credit card. Each tiny purchase builds the habit of clicking yes to the next one, and spending a dollar each time can add up to big bucks.

Free games can produce enormous profits. *Fortnite* made $1.2 billion in under a year by selling early access to game modes and new dances and skins (appearance options) for characters. To boost sales, the game uses limited-time offers to create a sense of urgency and exclusivity. About 70 percent of *Fortnite* players make in-game purchases, spending an average of $84.67 a year—more than the company could have made by selling a box copy of the game.

Although this profit model works well, it also raises ethical issues. Young players often don't understand how much money they're spending, as in the case of a seven-year-old boy who ran up a $6,000 bill in a single day playing *Jurassic World*. Companies including Facebook, Google, Apple, and Amazon have faced class-action lawsuits for making in-app purchases too easy for minors to make and too hard for adults to track. These cases have ended in huge settlements, with Amazon paying up to $70 million in refunds.

INVISIBLE DESIGN

To maximize profits, companies try to create apps that allow users to get started without instructions. "Good design is like a refrigerator," explains Irene Au, Google's former head designer. "When it works, no one notices, but when it doesn't, it sure stinks." Because people typically only think about a program's design when they're frustrated or confused, the best designs are "invisible."

Invisible design requires both time and skill, so large software development projects typically include many UX and UI designers. On small projects, developers often have to handle design decisions on their own. To create user-friendly programs, designers and developers follow several core principles:

Consistency. Designers keep users oriented by using consistent menus, screen layouts, colors, and fonts throughout their apps. So users have less to learn, designers rely on well-established standards, such as placing menus at the top of the screen and allowing touch screen users to zoom in by spreading their thumb and finger apart.

Simplicity. Designers make programs simple by avoiding information overload and making it easy for users to get things right. Help buttons should pop up essential information written in simple language instead of linking to a 200-page pdf full of techspeak. Video games should alert players with sounds and images when they're running low on health instead of expecting players to track that information.

Efficiency. Designers minimize the number of steps required for each task and create shortcuts for common tasks. Calendar apps often allow users to add a 15-minute reminder with a single tap rather than forcing them to type a specific time. Online checkouts often allow shoppers to click "shipping and billing addresses match" rather than making people enter their address twice.

Mistake proofing. Users inevitably make mistakes—people get confused or tap the wrong thing when their phone slips. UX designers build in features to protect people from making common mistakes. For example, they may automate file backups to protect people who forget to save their work. Because email users often forget to add attachments, Gmail scans for words such as *attached* and pops up a warning when users try to send the email without the promised file. Designers also make actions reversible so users can recover from mistakes.

Accessibility. Designers prioritize functionality over artistic elements to make programs accessible to people with visual, auditory, or physical disabilities. A tiny button may look cute but be hard for someone with shaky hands to use. To help people with visual impairments, designers choose large, clear fonts to enhance readability. They add text-based descriptions of pictures, called *alt-tags,* to images on websites, which can be read aloud by screen-reading programs. Instead of relying only on red text to highlight important information, designers add icons to catch the attention of people with color blindness.

Clarity. Designers use color, shape, size, and movement to guide users. Because humans' visual systems are drawn to centrally positioned, bright, and moving objects, or to a combination of those features, designers use those features to highlight key information. When they want to downplay information, they move it to the side or present it in gray. Because people read English from left to right, designers use right-pointing arrows to suggest next steps. They also draw on standard icons, such as a green check or a red "x," because users automatically understand their meaning.

Feedback. Designers reduce user anxiety by providing clear feedback, such as creating buttons that change color when pushed so users know their input was received. For time-consuming tasks, designers add status bars so that users know the program is working, not stalled. Although some status bars accurately indicate time remaining, others have a purely psychological purpose. The TurboTax do-it-yourself tax program pairs an artificial slowdown with an animated status bar claiming the program is checking for every possible tax break. The program doesn't actually need this time—the company added this unnecessary step to boost customer confidence. "Completing a tax return often has at least some level of stress and anxiety associated with it," explains TurboTax spokesperson Rob Castro. "To offset these feelings, we use a variety of design elements . . . to ensure our customers' peace of mind that their returns are accurate and they are getting all the money they deserve."

Developers, and even designers, often overestimate how user-friendly their programs are. Menus and procedures will make sense to the people who created them, even if they are likely to confuse everyone else. To account for that, designers may do hands-on testing with regular users, watching to see where people get stuck.

Entrepreneur Scotty Allen and UX designer Richard Littauer took this a step further, creating a design-review service called, "The User Is My Mom." For around $75, Scotty's mom will take a video of herself attempting to use an app or website. Pam Allen is no fool. She has a master's degree, speaks French fluently, and tutors college students. However, as a woman in her mid-60s, she is not a digital native and lacks the context of people who grew up using computers. "I just don't think to try what they do," she explains. "I don't often 'see' boxes or icons that are so obvious to younger people."

Her efforts quickly reveal bad design elements likely to frustrate or confuse users. As the business's marketing page says, "She can't understand your website and it isn't her fault."

ACTIVITY: USER EXPERIENCE

Choose a program you know well, such as a favorite video game or photo-editing app. Have people who have never used that app attempt to make sense of it. Can they get going without your help? Are options clear, or do they have to poke everything to figure out what it does? You may find patterns in how people respond, such as teenagers catching on more quickly than young children and older adults or frequent phone users being more likely to recognize the meaning of icons.

Next, try something new yourself. Download a free mobile app or try a free online program such as Google Earth. As you play around with it, what do you find confusing, distracting, or annoying? What changes would make it easier to use? Could the app do a better job with consistency, simplicity, efficiency, mistake proofing, accessibility, clarity, or feedback?

EXASPERATING DESIGN

In February 2018, Snapchat updated its user interface. It moved chats and stories to a new "Friends" page, changed the content-display algorithm, and introduced a "Discover" page filled with brand content. Angry users found the update confusing and overly commercialized. Over 1.2 million signed a Change.org petition called "Remove the New Snapchat Update."

DESIGN IN ACTION

In seventh grade, Amir Helmy began working with his father to create a seizure-detecting app. He'd been inspired by a family friend who was exploring ways to use wearable sensors to monitor her patient's seizures. Helmy realized those sensors resembled the built-in motion detectors in smartphones—software alone could turn a phone into a seizure-detecting device.

Over the next six years, Helmy and his father attracted $10,000 in funding on Indiegogo and won $75,000 in the Epilepsy Foundation Shark Tank Competition. The Helmys used those funds to develop the Seizario app, which detects abnormal movements and alerts emergency contacts to seizures and falls.

To make the app user-friendly, the Helmys followed core UX and UI principles. They gave each screen a consistent layout, using large fonts and high-contrast colors to make the app accessible for people with vision impairments. They made setup simple, guiding users through choosing motion-detection options and entering emergency contacts. The Helmys also took several steps to mistake-proof the app. To avoid confusion, they designed the app's home page to clearly indicate any fall and seizure-detection features the user had turned off. To prevent false alarms, they built in time to disable the emergency alert if someone had simply tripped or dropped their phone. They also added a manual alert option in case the app missed a mild seizure. To activate it, users flip a switch and tap the emergency button twice—easy, but unlikely to be triggered by shoving a phone into a pocket.

In 2018 the Association for Computing Machinery awarded Helmy the $10,000 Cutler-Bell Prize for high school students for his work on Seizario.

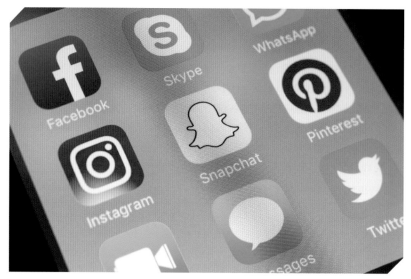

Even the addictive power of apps such as Snapchat can come second to the sway of celebrity opinion, such as that of Kylie Jenner.

Kylie Jenner, with almost 25 million Twitter followers, tweeted, "sooo does anyone else not open Snapchat anymore? Or is it just me . . . ugh this is so sad." As her tweet went viral, Snapchat's market value dropped by $1.3 billion.

Even before the unfortunate update, many users found Snapchat confusing. Instead of navigating with drop-down menus, Snapchat users swipe up, down, left, or right to access different screens. Jeremy Liew, Snapchat's first investor, considers this unconventional approach superior to traditional design.

Not everyone agrees. In his early attempts to use Snapchat, technology writer Will Oremus described himself as "flustered and sweating, haplessly punching runic symbols in a doomed bid to accomplish the basic task of viewing my friends' messages before they expire." He continued, "Snapchat, in short, makes me feel old."

That may be exactly the experience Snapchat wanted him to have. Facebook was created for college students, but young people left in droves once their parents started signing up. Snapchat's confusing user interface may help Snap Inc. avoid that. "Snapchat is notorious for making no sense to older users," writes marketing manager Hannah Alvarez. Unlike other apps, which offer tutorials, standardized icons, and detailed help menus, Snapchat simply drops people into the app. That approach may effectively keep out the "undesirables" (meaning people over the age of 25).

DARK DESIGN

Most bad design is accidental, but some designers use their expertise to manipulate people into making choices that go against their own interests. Dark design patterns weaponize UX and UI techniques to boost corporate profits.

Deceptive design. In the bait-and-switch approach, software tricks users by changing the meaning of common actions. In 2016 Microsoft used this tactic to push people into upgrading to Windows 10. For weeks, users saw pop-up boxes encouraging them to upgrade. Those who weren't interested clicked the "x" at the top of the box to close the pop-up and refuse the upgrade. Eventually, Microsoft changed the pop-up so that clicking "x" authorized the upgrade, angering many people who felt tricked into installing unwanted software.

Sketchy defaults. Default installation settings make it easy for inexperienced users to get started with a new program, but the settings often prioritize business interests over the users' best interests. Many free software programs make money by bundling the free software with a pop-up ad program. Savvy users can avoid it, but the standard installation sticks users with unwanted ads.

For most free apps, default settings allow the company to sell or share user data, which benefits the company, but not the user. When new European regulations required companies to let users opt out of data sharing, the blogging site Tumblr forced users to decline hundreds of data-sharing agreements individually. Since they could have offered a universal opt-out button, presumably the intent was to make opting out seem like too much of a hassle.

Persuasive formatting. In the persuasive formatting technique, designers use the size, color, and placement of objects to manipulate users. Free software sites trick people into clicking ads by hiding the link inside a brightly colored "Download now!" button in the center of the screen. They tuck the true download link in the corner where people won't find it until they've already clicked the ad.

Even the London Zoo used persuasive formatting to trick users into making a donation. On their ticket purchase page, clicking the large green arrow pointing right automatically added a 10 percent donation to the basket. To check out without making a donation, users had to find a small, colorless, backward-pointing arrow.

Hidden costs. Roach motel designs make it easy to get into a situation but hard to get out. Many websites make it easy to download and install a free software trial but have no online options for canceling. Users discover they have to spend hours calling an understaffed phone line to avoid a monthly service fee.

Australian airline Jetstar angered customers by defaulting to a five-dollar seat selection fee for online ticket purchases. Customers could accept a randomly assigned seat for free, but designers intentionally made that option difficult to find. Some online

BAD DESIGN LAUNCHED A PANIC

In a 2018 training exercise, the Hawai'i Emergency Management Agency accidentally texted, "BALLISTIC MISSILE THREAT INBOUND TO HAWAII. SEEK IMMEDIATE SHELTER. THIS IS NOT A DRILL." to every smartphone in Hawai'i. Panicked residents and tourists believed they were about to die. Some grabbed emergency supplies and headed to basements. Others simply gathered with family to be together at the end.

Badly designed software played a role in the fiasco. The alert-management screen showed users a disorganized jumble of test messages, drills, and real alerts, with no color or layout cues to help users distinguish among them. The inaccurate option selected that day, "PACOM (CDW) – STATE ONLY" appeared right below the option "1. TEST Message," making it easy to misread as the test option.

After an investigation, the agency fired the man who sent the alert. He denied selecting the wrong item out of confusion, accusing his coworkers of sloppy work that made him believe Hawai'i was truly under attack.

> .NG:
> e is no current ballistic missile threat. The
> rgency alert warning has been sounded by
> ake, according to Civil Defense.
>
> NSTAGRAM   17m
> ıst posted a photo.
>
> HNN   18m
> AKING:
> rgency alert issued to Hawaii phones: "Ballistic
> sile threat inbound to Hawaii. Seek immediate
> ter. This is not a drill."
>
> EMERGENCY ALERTS   29m
> rgency Alert

Thirty-eight minutes after the initial emergency alert, it was confirmed as a false alarm by the emergency alert system.

Regardless of what caused the mistake, bad software design made the problem worse. The system lacked common safeguards, such as having completely separate programs for drills and real alerts or requiring a second person to confirm alerts. Even worse, the software was built without any way to cancel an alert or send a message that people are safe. Technical staff addressed the issue in just 38 minutes—an impressive feat—but also a long time for the panicked residents of Hawai'i to wait.

retailers take a similar approach, automatically adding items to the checkout basket, such as insurance policies for items purchased. Since shoppers typically assume their cart only includes the items they added, the ploy tricks them into buying unnecessary junk.

Dark design can cross the line from manipulative to illegal. Stamps.com had to pay $2.5 million to settle a lawsuit because its "no-risk" trial set people up for a $15.99 monthly service charge. A court fined LinkedIn $13 million because its onboarding process used dark design patterns to trick new users into giving the company access to their contacts. LinkedIn then sent multiple emails inviting those contacts to join the career-networking site. Because the messages appeared to come directly from the user, the court ruled that the spammy-seeming emails could damage a person's professional reputation. In lawsuits against companies using deceptive design, lawyers may call UX or UI designers as expert witnesses to testify about whether a design violates common standards or appears likely to trick users.

123456: THE PSYCHOLOGY OF SECURITY

Rapper Kanye West made news during his White House visit when cameras live-broadcast him entering "000000" to unlock his iPhone. Although he was roundly mocked on social media, a surprising number of people have equally bad passwords. In 2017 a full 17 percent of people chose "123456" as their password, with "password" the next most popular choice. Other top choices were "football," "iloveyou," "welcome," "login," "monkey," and "starwars." About half of all people use one of the top 25 passwords, making life easy for hackers. Many others choose passwords based on pet names, birthdays, or favorite teams, information hackers can easily find on social media.

To thwart hackers, developers configure login systems to block access after several failed login attempts. Hackers get around that protection by cracking password files stolen from servers. Although these files are hashed (a form of encryption), hackers get unlimited password-cracking attempts.

Hackers have no difficulty cracking common passwords—hacking "123456" takes only 0.29 milliseconds with a program designed to try variations of common passwords. Other password-cracking programs take a "brute force" approach, cycling through every possible combination of letters, numbers, and symbols. These programs can test billions of passwords per second.

With brute force hacking programs, the shorter the password, the easier it is to hack. It doesn't matter if a person's password is cats123 or c1a2t3s. Both are seven characters long and will be cracked in about two seconds. Longer passwords are much harder to break. At 25 characters, "KanyeWestUsedABadPassword" would take six septillion years to crack, according to HowSecureIsMyPassword.net.

The strongest passwords are long, include numbers, symbols, and capital letters, and avoid dictionary words and repeated or sequential numbers. Because people forget random combinations of letters, numbers, and symbols, experts suggest adapting a memorable phrase to include misspellings and symbols. Instead of choosing common passwords like "monkey" or "starwars," people could start with the phrase "MonkeysLoveStarWars." They could make it more secure by adapting it to M*nkeysLuvSt@rW@rs? That will take five quintillion years to crack.

That said, telling people how to create secure passwords doesn't do much good. Despite educational campaigns, the list of terrible but common passwords has hardly changed over the years. In response, developers have tried the logical-seeming approach of forcing people to choose strong passwords and update them regularly.

Unfortunately, that tactic may actually decrease security. People forced to create complex passwords end up using a sticky note on their monitor to keep track of it. When users have to change passwords frequently, they "select weaker passwords to begin with, and then change them in predictable ways that attackers can guess easily," says security researcher Lorrie Cranor.

In fact, people react predictably to all password requirements. When developers require passwords to have a capital letters, people typically capitalize the first letter. Instead of "monkey," they choose "Monkey." When developers require a number, people slap a "1" at the end. Requiring a special character led to passwords with an "!" at the end. If forced to put a number within the word, "Monkey" becomes "MOnkey" or "Monk3y." During password updates, "Monkey1" consistently becomes "Monkey2" and "Monkey!" becomes "Monkey!!"

Because people respond so consistently to password requirements, password-cracking programs account for typical choices. According to Cranor, "All the complicated password policies don't prevent—or even really slow down—cracking of many users' passwords."

To improve security, developers need to understand that humans are illogical. Instead of trying to change people and their tendency to choose rotten passwords, many developers have started changing processes instead. Approaches such as dual-factor authentication make passwords less important because people must also provide some other proof of identity, such as a thumbprint or login code texted to their phone.

The need for developers to consider human psychology during software development goes far beyond security issues. Design decisions influence how much time and money people will spend on an app and whether people with disabilities will be able to access that app. That means design decisions are also ethical decisions. Rather than just figuring out *how* to get an app to work, developers need to consider the likely impact of the app and whether they *should* get it to work.

CHAPTER 6
SOFTWARE DEVELOPMENT ETHICS

As developers, we are often one of the last lines of defense against potentially dangerous and unethical practices," writes Bill Sourour. He learned this lesson the hard way in a job building websites for a marketing firm. One of Sourour's projects involved coding a know-your-treatment-options quiz for a pharmaceutical company. The quiz appeared on a website designed to look like an unbiased informational site for teenage girls. The catch was that no matter how girls answered quiz questions, the website almost always recommended the client's drug.

At the time, Sourour didn't feel especially troubled about creating a website intended to trick teenage girls—it just seemed like clever marketing. Then Sourour learned that one of the girls taking the drug had killed herself, perhaps because the drug's side effects included depression and suicidal tendencies. When he realized his teenage sister was also taking the drug, his role in that tragedy hit home. Sourour resigned from that job and committed himself to considering the implications of his code for all future work. He refers to his work on the drug website as "the code I'm still ashamed of," and urges developers to "take a stand and ensure that our ethics are ever-present in our code."

WITH GREAT POWER COMES GREAT RESPONSIBILITY

Because software plays a role in almost every area of life, ethical missteps can have serious consequences. In 2015 regulators discovered Volkswagen had used software to cheat on emissions tests, making 11 million diesel cars appear 40 times less polluting than they actually were. The software activated all the car's antipollution features during emissions tests but kept them off under normal driving conditions to boost performance. The fraud led to the CEO's arrest and cost Volkswagen billions of dollars in fines and repairs. Poor sales led to layoffs, leaving 30,000 people without jobs. Even worse, researchers calculated that the cars released enough extra pollution in the United States to contribute to the early deaths of 59 people. Developers may not have come up with the cheating scheme, but they did fail in their ethical obligations by carrying it out.

At Google, developers have begun pushing back on projects they consider unethical. For example, in China the government censors websites related to human rights, pro-democracy movements, and reports of violent police or military action against civilians. Google withdrew from China in 2010 to avoid involvement in censorship but in 2018 began working on Project Dragonfly, a search engine that censors results according to Chinese rules. Over 1,400 Google employees signed a letter protesting any return to the Chinese market, saying it violated the company's original motto, "Don't be evil."

Google employees also protested Project Maven, a Pentagon-funded contract to create artificial intelligence (AI) software capable of using drone surveillance to

CODE OF ETHICS

The Association for Computing Machinery (ACM) is a professional organization for computer scientists. Its code of ethics encourages developers to do the following:

- Prevent harm to people, property, and the environment.
- Correct accidental harm.
- Report harmful acts.
- Work within their area of competence.
- Avoid conflicts of interest.
- Encourage the fair participation of all people in the field and avoid harassment, bullying, and abuse of power.
- Develop inclusive technologies.
- Ensure software does not discriminate against any group.
- Respect copyright law.
- Protect confidential information by designing secure systems and promptly notifying victims of data breaches.

identify and track objects. That software would save soldiers thousands of tedious hours searching through drone videos for evidence of suspicious activity. However, it would also move the military closer to having an AI capable of making bombing decisions on its own. When news of Project Maven spread, a dozen employees resigned and over 4,000 employees petitioned Google to terminate the project. Outside Google, 1,200 researchers called for an international ban on weapon systems able to act independently, arguing that lethal military actions need human oversight. Due to the backlash, Google agreed to stop work on Project Maven when its contract expired in 2019. Google also released an AI code of ethics, promising to work only on projects that benefit society, avoid bias, and include adequate safety testing.

GARBAGE IN, GARBAGE OUT

"A computer is a stupid machine with the ability to do incredibly smart things, while computer programmers are smart people with the ability to do incredibly stupid things," says science writer Bill Bryson. "They are, in short, a dangerously perfect match."

What kinds of stupid things do computers and developers do together? Consider the car insurance algorithm that charged drunk drivers $1,500 less than excellent drivers with so-so credit or the hiring algorithm that gave higher scores to applicants who visited a specific manga website. Although computers churn through data at dizzying speeds, they cannot think. In these cases, developers "stupidly" put far too much confidence in machine learning.

In machine learning, developers feed vast quantities of information into programs, training them to recognize patterns in the data. Developers use this technique to produce decision-making *algorithms*—complex mathematical formulas that automate decisions, such as a bank's decision to approve a credit card application or loan someone money to buy a car.

To create a loan-making algorithm, developers would feed in old loan applications. The program would churn through the data to identify ways approved applications differed from rejected applications. Then the algorithm would use that information to make decisions about new applications. A typical loan algorithm would include an applicant's credit history, current income, outstanding debts, and bank balance, giving more weight to the most useful factors.

If developers use an unbiased data set, this process can produce a fair loan-making algorithm. However, if the original loan decisions discriminated against women or minorities (as has been the case throughout Europe and the United States), that bias will be baked into the final algorithm. Because gathering information about people is so easy now, many loan and credit algorithms include surprising factors such as an applicant's zip code, the number of grammatical errors in their social media posts, their friends' credit scores, and the places they shop. Those factors can work against financially responsible people living in low-income communities, who get dinged for shopping in nearby discount stores or having broke friends.

With machine learning, feeding flawed information into the program guarantees a bad outcome. Developers refer to this concept as garbage in, garbage out. The concept was illustrated perfectly in 2016 when Microsoft used Twitter to train an AI chatbot called Tay. Because people flooded Tay's feed with offensive tweets, within 16 hours Tay went from "can I just say that im stoked to meet u? humans are super cool" to spewing racist, pro-Hitler comments. Problems with Tay were so obvious that Microsoft quickly deleted Tay's tweets and took the offensive chatbot offline—issue solved with no lasting harm done. Unfortunately, many decision-making algorithms operate behind the scenes, making identifying the problems they cause much more difficult.

Many people believe that chatbots have the potential to be sophisticated personal assistants. However, there are still many issues to work out before such technology can become widespread, such as teaching AIs to interpret a user's tone of voice.

WEAPONS OF MATH DESTRUCTION

Virtually all Fortune 500 companies use résumé-screening software. Then algorithms, not people, reject many job applications. That time-saving approach becomes unjust if the algorithms have built-in biases against some groups of people. Presumably, no developers set out to create unfair algorithms, but machine learning makes them easy to create accidentally.

Developers train résumé-screening programs based on past hiring decisions and the success of current employees, which means any past injustice leads to future injustice. At companies such as Apple, Facebook, Google, and Microsoft, about 75 percent of people in technical roles are male, making it likely that algorithms will be biased toward male hires. The challenges of avoiding that bias became clear when Amazon used a decade's worth of job applications to create a résumé-screening AI. Although Amazon tested 500 different approaches to screening résumés, it couldn't create an unbiased program. The program gave lower scores to graduates of women's colleges and résumés including the word *women*. It gave higher scores to résumés with verbs such as *executed* and *captured*, which were more common among male applicants but didn't reflect superior skills. Ultimately, Amazon concluded the software actively discriminated against women and abandoned it entirely in 2017.

Although the internet contains the full wealth of human knowledge, biased algorithms can distort the information people find. Search engine and advertising algorithms serve up content based on a person's age, sex, location, and search history, which means some people see only a sliver of the options available. Job-hunting women see only one in six of the ads for high-paying positions shown to men. People living in low-income communities see far more ads from shady payday lenders than people living in wealthier neighborhoods. Biased algorithms can also perpetuate extremism and misinformation. When people with fringe political views or faith in bogus miracle cures search online, algorithms prioritize sites similar to the ones they've visited in the past. Seeing top search results that align with their skewed worldview makes it easier for them to conclude that their views are accurate and mainstream.

Algorithms may even have swayed the 2016 presidential election. Clickbait stories generate more advertising revenue than dry news stories, so algorithms populate news feeds with whatever people are most likely to read. In the months before the election, Facebook's algorithms promoted fake news stories critical of candidate Hillary Clinton.

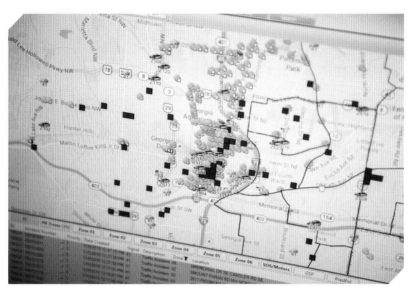

This map of Atlanta, Georgia, produced by PredPol, shows where the software predicts there to be more crime. Each of the colored squares represents an area of 500 square feet (46 sq. m), and the red squares indicate "hot boxes," or areas predicted to experience more crime.

Researchers estimate these stories cost Clinton 2 percent of the vote in battleground states. Because she lost those states by less than a percentage point, profit-maximizing algorithms may have cost her the election.

Decision-making algorithms have become so common that results from one algorithm often feed into another. Over time, this amplifies the impact of unfair decisions, with a slight bias in the first algorithm potentially leading to significant bias at the end of the decision-making chain. The effect of interactions between algorithms has become an especially important issue in the field of criminal justice. Predictive policing algorithms suggest useful areas for police to patrol based on factors such as arrest rates, crime reports, population density, and the location of bars. These algorithms tend to direct police to patrol low-income and minority communities. Having more officers in those communities leads to higher arrest rates for low-level, nonviolent crimes such as drug use or loitering (which rarely lead to arrests in wealthy neighborhoods).

Those arrests feed back into the predictive policing algorithm, which tells police to keep patrol rates high in that neighborhood, leading to yet more arrests. The arrests also feed forward into parole, probation, and criminal-sentencing algorithms. Besides using an offender's criminal record to make recommendations, those algorithms draw on factors beyond the offender's control, such as having a parent or friend with an arrest record. This means that people living in heavily policed areas get higher risk scores for the same crime than people living in other neighborhoods. Often those high-risk scores translate to harsher sentences.

Because badly designed algorithms can have life-changing effects, data scientist Cathy O'Neil calls them "weapons of math destruction." To combat the problem, she founded a company to help ensure algorithms are effective and unbiased.

Ethical developers can prevent unfair algorithms by using unbiased data sets for

ETHICS OF SELF-DRIVING CARS

Algorithms guide every action taken by a self-driving car, from staying within a lane to maintaining a safe distance from other cars. Although the goals of those algorithms may seem simple, they raise many ethical dilemmas.

The most obvious dilemma involves handling unavoidable collisions. Should the car minimize loss of life overall or prioritize the safety of

A self-driving car in action

its passengers over pedestrians? Should children's lives be valued over those of elderly people? Human drivers make those decisions on the spot. For self-driving cars, someone writing code in a cubicle will determine what happens when a car cannot safely avoid a child who has darted into the street. Will the car swerve right toward a tree, potentially killing its passenger? Swerve left into an oncoming vehicle? Brake but continue driving straight?

Other ethical dilemmas are more subtle. Slowing to 20 miles (32 km) per hour in residential areas would protect pedestrians but annoy passengers who want to go the speed limit of 25 miles (40 km) per hour. Acceleration, turning, and braking algorithms could prioritize either speed or minimizing pollutant emissions. Although that may not seem like an ethical decision, every year pollution contributes to 9,500 early deaths in London alone.

machine learning and by writing code that limits what a program can do. For example, after their failed chatbot experiment, Microsoft developers added code to block offensive words from the vocabulary of future chatbots. Google has tweaked search algorithms to keep factually incorrect Holocaust-denial sites from appearing as top search results.

ACTIVITY: YOU MAKE THE CALL

Although experts believe self-driving cars will reduce accidents, they cannot prevent them entirely. Developers need to specify what cars should do when injury to humans is inevitable.

Describe the rules you would have a car follow, taking into account the number of people injured, the age of victims, the severity of likely injuries, property damage, and any other factor you consider important.

Different companies are likely to make different choices about how self-driving cars respond when harm is unavoidable. One company might program cars to protect passengers at all costs, prioritizing the life of the car's owner over other lives in the car. Another company might program cars to save the most lives possible and to prioritize children over adults, without any preference for passengers over pedestrians.

PRIVACY FOR SALE

Each minute, humanity watches 4.1 million YouTube videos, and sends 156 million emails, 16 million texts, and half a million pictures on Snapchat. While we entertain ourselves, companies harvest data. They mine that data to understand our behavior and desires, and translate that understanding into more effective ad campaigns.

In 2014 a company allegedly doing academic research paid people to download a Facebook app and complete a personality test. That app took advantage of a programming loophole to collect data on 87 million Facebook friends of the test-takers. Cambridge Analytica, a political consulting firm, used psychological profiles created using that Facebook data to tailor campaign ads to individuals. Those targeted ads encouraged Americans to elect Donald Trump president and encouraged United Kingdom residents to vote to leave the European Union. No one knows how effective the ads were, but the scandal woke people up to the vast amount of data companies have collected.

Journalist Aja Romano explained, "Cambridge Analytica didn't 'hack' our internet usage and our Facebook information so much as exploit the way the system was naturally designed to work." Facebook knew app developers could access extensive user data and made it easy for companies to target ads based on age, sex, ethnicity, location, political orientation, and interests. Many critics felt Facebook executives had valued profit over ethics.

Concern about Facebook's weak privacy policies led to a $37 billion drop in the company's value and an international movement to quit Facebook. Although Facebook has tightened access to its data, many apps can still access people's profiles, photos, videos, posts, and friends. For its own purposes, Facebook records every login time, location, and device. Facebook tracks search histories, likes, and comments. It knows which games and apps people use, what music they play, what movies they like, and which ads they have clicked. Facebook also merges that information with data from Instagram and apps people sign in to with their Facebook logins. With 1.8 billion active Facebook users and 800 million Instagram users, that translates to an immense amount of data.

Facebook is not alone—corporations make billions in profit each year from selling user data. The business models for "free" apps such as Snapchat, Pinterest, Instagram, Google, and Bing all depend on user data. Google doesn't give away email accounts, photo and document storage, word-processing software, translation tools, mapping programs, and a search engine to be nice. These services help Google boost profits by targeting advertisements more effectively.

Google stores every search a person has ever done. It knows which apps and extensions people use, which sites they have bookmarked, where they have shopped, who they connect with on social media, and what they stream on YouTube. Google knows where people have traveled and how long they stayed there. Journalist Dylan Curran points out, "We would never let the government or a corporation put cameras or microphones in our homes or location trackers on us. But we just went ahead and did it ourselves because—to hell with it!—I want to watch cute dog videos!"

Individuals can take steps to protect their data. Some people avoid social media apps entirely and choose search engines such as DuckDuckGo that don't store users'

search histories. Others use apps and search engines that sell data but set their accounts to the most restrictive data-sharing settings.

Developers can also take steps to help protect user data. Although few developers have a say in their employer's profit model, any developer can choose not to work for companies that profit by selling user data. Within a company that sells user data, developers can advocate for ethical software designs, such as making it easy for users to change privacy settings. Alternatively, developers could join start-ups experimenting with new ways of making money. For example, with Datacoup and Permission.io, users control the type of information companies collect about their online behavior and share in the profits from selling that data.

The ethical implications of big data expand far beyond the role of developers, because companies buying data can easily gain access to personal information. Although companies usually strip names from the data sets they sell, sophisticated data-combination programs can easily reattach names to data by merging data sets.

KNOW YOUR VALUE

Not all user data has equal value. Companies command higher rates for data on big spenders. Data from a healthy, married, apartment-dwelling American sells for about 20 cents. However, if that person were recently engaged (and likely to plan an expensive wedding) or pregnant (and in need of baby gear), their data is worth an extra 10 cents. Home ownership and expensive hobbies also increase the value of data by 10 cents. Expensive health conditions, such as diabetes and back pain, boost value by 15 cents. Those numbers might seem small, but data doesn't go bad or get used up. Companies can sell millions of people's data as many times as they want.

Companies also make money by targeting ads to users. In 2017 Facebook earned an average of $1.72 for each ad click. Google earned an average of $2.32. Researchers estimate that an individual's personal data generates up to $290 each year for the advertising industry.

Hackers selling black market data make even more. Netflix login information runs about $3. An Amazon login goes for almost $9. A usable credit card number sells for around $25. A full set of data including passwords, a driver's license number, and banking information nets hackers at least $300.

That creates the risk of a world in which health insurance companies raise rates for people whose social media posts suggest depression or employers reject candidates who recently shopped for pregnancy tests. In countries that restrict freedom of speech, political beliefs, sexual orientation, or religious practice, the power of big data may be life-threatening. As access to personal data expands, people working for many different types of organizations will need to consider whether a convenient or profitable use of data is ethical.

MALICIOUS SOFTWARE

In 2017 WannaCry ransomware infected over 300,000 computers in 150 countries, including computers at hospitals, government agencies, and manufacturers. People lost all access to their files and were left with nothing but a screen reading, "Ooops, your files have been encrypted!" Without access to key medical information, hospitals in the United Kingdom had to cancel appointments and close emergency departments. WannaCry also disrupted FedEx, Chinese government agencies, a German railway firm, a French car manufacturer, and the Russian postal service.

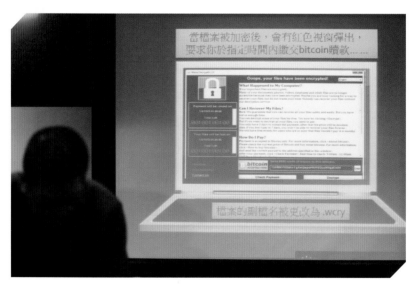

This photo from a press conference in Wan Chai, Hong Kong, shows what a computer displays when infected with WannaCry ransomware.

The WannaCry attackers offered decryption services to people who paid a $300 bitcoin ransom within three days or a $600 ransom within a week. After that, hackers would delete files forever. Based on the advice of security experts, few companies paid the ransom. Those that did never regained access to their files. WannaCry cost companies billions.

Even unsuccessful attacks carry a real cost. Large financial institutions and government agencies spend about $5 million apiece each year fighting malware and data breaches. Utility companies spend about $3 million a year on security. That level of investment is essential—successful attacks carry an average cost of $1.3 million, and most companies face over 100 attacks each year.

No one disputes that the WannaCry attack was an unethical, criminal act. However, people have debated the ethics of choices made by the National Security Agency (NSA), which inadvertently made the attack possible. Hackers based the WannaCry ransomware on EternalBlue, a hacking tool developed by the NSA to take advantage of a Windows security issue. Reports suggest the NSA spent five years exploiting that

BACKDOORS

Even with 3,500 security engineers, Microsoft cannot identify every risk before releasing new software. Companies have to balance security risks against time, cost, and convenience. To make troubleshooting and maintenance easier, developers sometimes create undocumented entry routes into programs called *backdoors*. Typically, only a program's creators know about these secret, password-protected access points. If hackers discover a backdoor, they can use it to alter the program or steal information.

In 2013 a leak of secret documents revealed that American and British intelligence agencies had pressured makers of data encryption software to build backdoors for them. These entry points gave agencies access to information they wouldn't have been able to decrypt. Companies had to decide whether the benefits of helping intelligence agencies outweighed privacy concerns and the risk of making their programs worthless if hackers discovered the access point.

vulnerability, rather than reporting it to Microsoft. They only revealed the security issue after hackers stole EternalBlue. Microsoft released a security patch quickly, but many organizations were slow to install it, making them easy targets for WannaCry.

The WannaCry attack wasn't the first time code written with good intentions ended up causing problems. In 2009 the Stuxnet computer worm sabotaged uranium enrichment facilities in Iran by causing some equipment to run dangerously fast for short periods. The excessive speed ruined equipment, forcing the plant to replace thousands of expensive machines and spend countless hours troubleshooting.

Evidence suggests American and Israeli intelligence agencies developed Stuxnet to derail Iran's attempts to develop nuclear weapons. The worm did slow progress and drive up costs. But it also established the idea that peacetime cyberattacks on other countries are okay. Since then the US has suffered such attacks, including a series of cyberattacks on American banks. Because Stuxnet got out in the world, anyone can obtain the code, which cybersecurity expert Sean McGurk calls a "textbook on how to attack key US installations." With minor modifications, hackers could use the code to attack nuclear reactors, chemical plants, water treatment plants, the electrical grid, or natural gas pipelines.

HACKTIVISM

Hackers typically break into computer systems to make money. But *hacktivists* (activist hackers) are vigilantes, infiltrating systems to work for social change. Major hacktivist groups include Anonymous, Cult of the Dead Cow, WikiLeaks, and LulzSec. Although most hacktivist groups are loose collectives with no clear leader, their actions have had significant political and social impacts.

Chaos Computer Club was one of the earliest hacktivist groups. In the 1980s, it notified the German post office about cybersecurity vulnerabilities. When the agency insisted its system was secure, the club stole a significant amount of money to make its point. To demonstrate its good intent, the club returned the money a day later.

Cult of the Dead Cow paved the way for other hacktivists by creating software used to encrypt messages, seek out web server vulnerabilities, and launch distributed denial-of-service (DDoS) attacks. A DDoS attack is designed to shut down a computer, network, or website by using multiple systems to flood it with more information or requests than the targeted system can handle. In the late 1990s, the Cult of the Dead

Cow helped Chinese citizens access government-censored information. However, the cult's tools have also been used in harmful hacks.

Anonymous has been one of the most active groups. It has taken down child pornography websites, outed members of the Ku Klux Klan, shut down 5,000 pro-terrorism Twitter accounts, and launched DDoS attacks against ISIS web pages. Although its anti-terrorism actions have been illegal, Anonymous, by its actions, prompted the United Kingdom security minister to declare himself "grateful for any of those who are engaged in the battle against this kind of wickedness."

MALWARE TYPES

Malware, short for malicious software, includes any software intended to do harm. People may deploy malware to make money, steal information, attract attention, or get revenge. Malware comes in many forms.

- *Viruses* infect other files, spreading within and across computers. They may damage operating systems or destroy files.
- *Worms* infect networks, using one infected machine to target others. *Botnets* are infected networks controlled by hackers, who use the botnet to send spam or overwhelm websites with DDoS attacks.
- A *Trojan horse* disguises itself as an update or legitimate software. Rather than wreaking havoc, Trojans quietly steal passwords or open access points for other malware programs.
- *Spyware* monitors a computer user's behavior, tracking keystrokes and app use to steal passwords or credit card numbers. Legitimate versions allow parents or employers to monitor computer use.
- *Ransomware* hijacks a computer, threatening to destroy all files unless the computer owner pays a ransom.
- *Adware* delivers a relentless stream of unwanted ads, distracting users and making computers sluggish.

During the Arab Spring uprising, citizens across the Middle East protested government corruption and human rights abuses. Governments attempted to quell protests by limiting protesters' ability to organize and communicate with the outside world. In response, hacktivist groups launched cyberattacks on the governments of Syria, Egypt, and Tunisia, restored access to blocked news sites, and helped protesters post updates to social media.

Although most hacktivism breaks the law, people disagree about whether illegal acts are also unethical. Some people consider any DDoS attack a criminal act. Others consider socially motivated attacks a form of civil disobedience, like a digital sit-in. The ACM Code of Ethics and Professional Conduct clearly prohibits malicious hacking but offers a hint of wiggle room for unauthorized access based on a "compelling belief that it is consistent with the public good."

In the science and tech world, some people consider hacktivist Alexandra Elbakyan a digital Robin Hood. Elbakyan, a Kazakhstani developer, was frustrated that most scientific journal articles cost a lot of money to read, limiting people's access to scientific discoveries. Because most research is government-funded, this struck Elbakyan as unfair. So she swiped pdfs of 64 million articles and made them available for free on Sci-Hub. Journalists have called her science's pirate queen. Scientists have downloaded millions of free articles. Unsurprisingly, publishers have been far less enthusiastic, responding to her hacktivism with lawsuits.

Ethical decisions are often complicated. Reasonable people disagree about where to draw the line on hacktivism, the sale of personal data, or allowing government agencies to create potentially dangerous software. Because software can have life-changing implications for people, colleges have started adding ethics classes to computer science majors. In addition to considering the ethical implications of *how* software is designed, the tech industry has also started thinking about ethical issues related to *who* is doing the designing. Software development teams made up of young, well-off, able-bodied, white men may be more likely to overlook the risks their new algorithm poses for people from different backgrounds.

CHAPTER 7
DIVERSITY IN COMPUTER SCIENCE

In 2018 the @coding.engineer Instagram account shared an image of Lyndsey Scott, a former Calvin Klein and Victoria's Secret model and current software developer. The post, "Coding Is for Anyone," listed the programming languages she uses.

Although some comments were positive, many were outright insulting, implying that a model couldn't possibly be a real developer. Scott, who had heard all this before, came to her own defense, noting that she graduated from Amherst College with a double major in computer science and theater and now works as a lead iOS developer. She has also helped over 1.3 million people by answering technical questions on Stack Overflow.

Scott described herself as an awkward and nerdy high school student but said that since she became a model, "many people are shocked to find out that I'm anything other than an airhead." As a developer, she has faced programmers who assumed she wouldn't be interested in

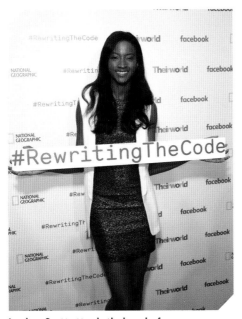

Lyndsey Scott attends the launch of #RewritingTheCode, a campaign to bring attention to the social disadvantages women and girls face from even before birth, and to empower girls to pursue their goals.

Isis Anchalee poses with a message for skeptics. Her hashtag, #iLookLikeAnEngineer, challenges people's stereotypes about software engineers.

technical conversations, avoided having her on their team, or talked about her as if she was just learning to code.

Although her appearance and previous work as a fashion model may be one reason people make assumptions about her brains, Scott sees this as a problem faced by all women in computer science. In an interview with Refinery29, she talked about the persistent failure to take women seriously. "If someone doesn't look like the image that people have in their mind of the conventional programmer," said Scott, "they often have to do more to prove them false."

Scott isn't alone in her experience. Software engineer Isis Anchalee was featured in a recruitment ad for her employer, OneLogin. The ad went viral on social media, with many commenters accusing the company of hiring a model instead of featuring a real developer. In response, Anchalee helped launch the #iLookLikeAnEngineer campaign, encouraging people who didn't fit the developer stereotype to post selfies. Within a day, 26,000 people of all ages and ethnicities had used the hashtag on Twitter, posting pictures of themselves wearing everything from evening gowns to hijabs.

BUSTING STEREOTYPES

A 2018 Google search for "Why are programmers so . . ." offered auto-complete suggestions of "rude," "weird," "arrogant," "awkward," and "smart," reflecting the common view of developers as geeky guys with poor social skills.

Media representations often reinforce that stereotype. On-screen, programmers are often nerdy loners coding obsessively in a basement surrounded by action figures and empty Mountain Dew cans. Even favorable portrayals are wildly inaccurate, since very few developers are boy geniuses running tech empires or edgy hackers capable of taking over government satellites.

Unfortunately, one stereotype about developers remains true—most developers are white men. In 2017 African Americans made up 11 percent of the US workforce but held only 7 percent of computer science jobs. Representation was even worse for Hispanic Americans, who made up 16 percent of the workforce but held only 7 percent of computer science jobs.

In most other STEM fields, representation by women has increased rapidly over the last decades. Women now fill 39 percent of physical science jobs, 46 percent of math-related jobs, and 75 percent of health-related STEM positions. Computer science is the only STEM field in which women's participation has decreased over time. In the 1960s, between 30 and 50 percent of programmers were women. That number fell to 25 percent by 2018.

Underrepresentation of women and people of color in computer science starts early. In 2017 girls took over half of all Advanced Placement (AP) exams , but girls took less than a quarter of AP computer science exams the same year. Only 13 percent of AP computer science students were Black or Latinx. That lack of representation carries over into college, where computer science majors are 82 percent men and 82 percent white.

The issue isn't that only white guys like programming or have the ability to write code. Asian, African, and Middle Eastern countries have many female developers. In India, 55 percent of computer science majors are women. Bob Martin, an expert developer who sees gender imbalance as a major problem, asks, "Where did all the women go? What's wrong with us that we are repelling half the people in the world?" The answer seems to involve a combination of social factors that shape who studies computer science and who chooses to stay in the field.

THE FIRST COMPUTERS BECAME THE FIRST PROGRAMMERS

Before "computer" referred to an electronic device, it was the job description for people performing complex mathematical calculations by hand. During World War II (1939–1945), computers were female mathematicians creating firing tables—detailed tables listing all the information soldiers needed to aim ballistic weapons. Tables needed to cover a thousand possible trajectories, accounting for such factors as distance, elevation, artillery weight, wind, temperature, and humidity. Even with 100 women working six days a week, computers didn't have enough time to do all the calculations required.

Gloria Ruth Gordon (*left*) and Ester Gerston wire a new program into the ENIAC.

In 1945 the army hired six computers to work on a secret firing-table calculating machine. The Electronic Numerical Integrator and Computer (ENIAC) filled a 50-foot-long (15 m) room with its 40 plug boards, 18,000 vacuum tubes, and thousands of 10-way switches.

Because this was a new creation, there was no user's guide. Computers Jean Bartik, Betty Holberton, Kay Antonelli, Marlyn Meltzer, Fran Spence, and Ruth Teitelbaum figured out how to program ENIAC by physically rearranging cables and flipping switches. The web of connections they created broke calculations down into small steps ENIAC could handle.

When the army unveiled ENIAC to the public in 1946, it could calculate a missile's trajectory in under 20 seconds. The men who developed ENIAC became famous, but the women who programmed it remained unknown for decades. That changed in the 1980s, when Harvard undergraduate Kathy Kleiman stumbled across photos of unnamed women operating ENIAC. Thanks to the years Kleiman spent tracking down and publicizing their stories, in 1997 all six programmers were inducted into the Women in Technology Hall of Fame.

DIGITAL DIVIDE

In the 1940s and 1950s, computer programming began to emerge as a profession. Although women were far from achieving equality in the workplace at that time, many of the first programmers were women. Programming was seen as tedious, detail-oriented work, and appropriate for female assistants to men doing the higher-status work of creating computers. Despite the lack of respect for their work, women were responsible for many of the earliest programming innovations. Their participation in the field of computer science rose steadily until the mid-1980s, when it suddenly dropped off.

Researchers link the disappearance of women in the field to the growing availability of personal computers in the late 1970s and early 1980s. Families often bought home computers to play video games. Because boys were slightly more likely to play the games and spend time on computers, computer manufacturers began targeting their marketing efforts at boys. Parents bought more computers for sons than for daughters and popular culture soon began to reflect the idea that computers were for boys. Movies cast boys and men as hackers, video games created male lead characters, and high school coding clubs filled with more boys than girls.

Before personal computers were popular, college students taking introductory coding classes all started at the same novice level. Once home computers became common, students who grew up using computers had a head start. Professors expected "intro" students to arrive knowing how to code, making classes intimidating for true beginners. Because more boys than girls had experimented with coding as

The PCjr was an affordable version of IBM's PC, the first so-called personal computer. It was aimed at the ordinary consumer, but it was more expensive than its competitors, the Apple II and the Commodore 64, and so IBM ceased production in 1985.

high school students, many girls entered classes at a disadvantage. So did students from lower-income backgrounds who were less likely to have had access to expensive personal computers. Relatively quickly, the makeup of computer science classes shifted toward white men from middle- and upper-class families.

That shift made women and people of color even less likely to major in computer science—it feels uncomfortable to walk into classrooms where the students and professors don't look like you. If a white guy in a computer science class asks a dumb question or fails a test, no one concludes white men can't handle the subject. If one of the few women or people of color in the class make a mistake, people may assume the entire group they represent just can't keep up.

Unfortunately, barriers in early access to coding opportunities are not just historical. In a 2018 Pew Research Center report, over two-thirds of STEM professionals identified poor educational access, lack of role models, and discrimination as barriers to diversity. Although computers have gotten more affordable, Americans in rural and low-income communities still have less access to computers, coding classes, and the internet. This gap between the haves and have-nots is the *digital divide*.

WHO'S ONLINE?

Overall, Americans have a high rate of internet access compared to the world average of 51 percent. However, wealthy, white, and suburban families have greater access than other groups. Lack of access limits opportunities to learn to code and may contribute to the tech industry's diversity problems.

HOUSEHOLDS WITH BROADBAND INTERNET ACCESS IN 2019

TYPE OF HOUSEHOLD	PERCENT
White Americans	79
African Americans	57
Hispanic Americans	61
Suburban households	79
Rural households	63
Households with incomes above $75,000	92
Households with incomes below $30,000	56

Although wealthy high schools typically offer programming classes, only 40 percent of US schools offer even one computer science class. Less than a quarter of schools with AP classes offer AP computer science. As a result, most students have to learn to code outside of school, and this puts kids who can't afford special camps and classes at a disadvantage. That matters, because students who take AP computer science are far more likely to major in computer science than students who do not.

BIAS AT WORK

Increasing diversity requires more than just getting women and people of color to major in computer science. The field suffers from a "leaky pipeline," a metaphor used to describe the reality that women are twice as likely as men to leave tech jobs. Of women who majored in computer science, only 38 percent end up working in the field.

Women and people of color don't leave because they dislike coding. According to a report from the Center for Talent Innovation, women leave because they feel shut out of key roles or undermined by their peers and bosses. For example, female developers describe being mistaken for the receptionist or expected to handle tasks male developers don't do, such as taking notes, fetching coffee, and cleaning up after meetings. Although women in computer science have higher salaries than women in general, they still earn only 87 cents for every dollar paid to men in similar roles. Similarly, Latinx and African American developers earn less than white developers.

These problems don't just arise for a few people. In 2016 a group of female executives released the Elephant in the Valley survey, which asked women with over a decade of experience in high-level tech jobs to describe their experiences. Two-thirds of the women surveyed described being excluded from networking opportunities. Almost all had faced demeaning comments from male colleagues and had clients turn to men with questions that should have been addressed to them.

In the 2018 Pew Research Center survey, three-quarters of women in computer science reported facing gender discrimination at work. People of color had similar experiences, with 62 percent of black people, 42 percent of Hispanic people, and 44 percent of Asian people in STEM fields reporting workplace discrimination. Many felt worn down by assumptions that they were lazy or had limited ability. Women of color in tech have an even more difficult path, since they may face negative stereotypes about their gender and their ethnicity.

PINKIFICATION

Some well-intentioned attempts to welcome girls and women into tech have played on limiting stereotypes. Sponsors have advertised events with fancy purple fonts, decorated with pink sequins, and offered goody bags filled with nail files and mirrors. Critics call this the *pinkification of STEM*.

Many girls and women feel insulted by the suggestion that they need girly elements to tempt them into technology. "Is it assumed that I will only be interested in rebuilding the infrastructure of this nation via civil engineering if there is some sort of glittery pink aspect involved?" asked high school senior Abby Wheat in an essay reacting to pinkified recruitment materials. "Do people really think that the only way you will ever get a girl to write coding for innovative software is to stick a butterfly somewhere in there?"

Emily Reid, curriculum director for Girls Who Code, explained, "The problem comes with assuming girls won't be inherently interested in computer science—that things like 'pink and princesses' are needed to lure them in." Instead, the magic lies in showing girls that they can use computer science to address problems they care about. Compared to men, women in STEM fields are almost twice as likely to value having a job focused on helping others. Rather than adding pink, organizations should highlight ways women can use software to improve education, health care, and social justice.

These reports of discrimination aren't just opinions—women and people of color in tech face real obstacles. Many studies show that women and people of color are perceived as having less scientific and technical ability. That bias can shape everything from who is hired to how their work is evaluated.

For example, in one experiment, scientists evaluated job applications for a lab manager position. The applications were identical except for the candidate's name. Half had a male name, and half had a female name. Scientists rated the "male" applicants as more competent, expressed more interest in mentoring them, and proposed starting salaries averaging almost $4,000 higher than for the "female" applicants.

Software developer bethanye McKinney Blount describes a career filled with men assuming she didn't know what she was doing. When she worked for Second Life as a senior software engineer, a male job applicant treated the questions she and a female vice president asked like jokes. Because Second Life quickly realized it did not want to

Women, particularly women of color, are underrepresented across most software development jobs. However, many individuals, organizations, and companies are tackling this issue head-on.

hire this disrespectful applicant, the company sent in a junior-level male developer so he could practice conducting job interviews. The foolish candidate reacted eagerly to a male presence, saying, "Finally, somebody who knows what's going on!"

Blount, who describes herself as a "remover-of-obstacles" on her LinkedIn profile, has responded by becoming one of many people working to eliminate bias in tech. She has played a major role in founding two companies—Compaas, which helps businesses make fair compensation decisions, and Project Include, which helps companies improve diversity.

A famous saying describes female ballroom dancers as doing everything men do but backward and in high heels. Journalist Liza Mundy updated that saying for the tech industry. She said, "It's more like doing everything backwards and in heels while some guy is trying to yank at your dress, and another is telling you that a woman can't dance as well as a man, oh, and could you stop dancing for a moment and bring him something to drink?"

Instead of staying in an unwelcoming environment, many women and people of color opt to take their talents to other fields. That decision doesn't just hurt the individual upending their career; lack of diversity leads directly to flawed software.

WHY DIVERSE PERSPECTIVES MATTER

In August 2017, Google engineer James Damore posted a document arguing that Google's efforts to train and recruit people from underrepresented groups discriminated against white men. He suggested that women were innately less interested in

WELCOMING ENVIRONMENTS

Many environments broadcast cues about the type of person who belongs, such as the pounding club music in a clothing store that encourages middle-aged shoppers to go elsewhere. In the workplace, everything from recruitment ads to office design can influence who feels welcome. Research shows women tend to avoid applying to jobs when advertisements emphasize stereotypically masculine traits. To solve that problem, some companies have started using gender-neutral descriptions of ideal candidates. For example, instead of seeking "aggressive code ninjas" or "powerful leaders who thrive on competition" they look for "exceptional programmers" and "goal-oriented mentors." These simple wording changes help boost the number and diversity of applicants.

tech work and less skilled at it, so trying to increase their numbers at Google was totally misguided.

Shortly thereafter, Google fired Damore. Danielle Brown, Google's vice president of diversity, integrity & governance, wrote, "We are unequivocal in our belief that diversity and inclusion are critical to our success as a company." But why try to increase diversity in computer science? If women and people of color aren't choosing tech careers, why try to lure them in?

From a business perspective, one good answer is that diversity boosts profits and spurs innovative thinking. "Diversity enhances creativity," explains Columbia business school professor Katherine Phillips. "It encourages the search for novel information and perspectives, leading to better decision making and problem solving." Companies with more diversity at the executive level make more money. With lower-level employees, having diverse teams predicts stronger performance and lower costs.

Diverse groups are also better at recognizing the range and complexity of problems. Teams made of all young, white, straight, male, or able-bodied developers may overlook issues obvious to others. Sheri Atwood, a single mother, developed SupportPay to help families reduce postdivorce conflict. The app helps separated parents track shared expenses and coordinate child support payments. Potential investors repeatedly questioned whether she had really written the code and suggested she hire a young guy to handle the tech side of things. Instead, Atwood pointed out that overreliance on young male developers has limited the range of apps available, saying, "The reason why there's no solution on the market today is because this isn't a 21-year-old-kid-in-a-hoodie problem."

It is easy for people to be oblivious to issues that don't affect them. Developers with typical vision choose color schemes that don't work for people with color blindness. Right-handed developers fail to realize that left-handers handle phones differently. When developers created the original code for uploading iPhone videos to YouTube, 10 percent of users ended up with upside-down videos. The development team eventually realized they hadn't considered that left- and right-handers rotate their phones in opposite directions.

Many software design decisions overlook women's needs. The original Apple Health app, which tracked everything from micronutrient intake to heart rate, offered no way to track menstrual cycles. Phone-based activity trackers were designed for people who keep phones in their pocket. Men typically do, but women's clothing often lack pockets large enough to hold a phone, causing trackers to underestimate their activity levels. Even phones themselves may work less well for women. As screen sizes have increased, phones have gotten harder for people with small hands to use. In an often-forwarded blog post, professor Zeynep Tufekci noted that she cannot type, take pictures, scroll, unlock, or even turn on her phone one-handed—something she sees men do all the time.

As Apple became aware of these issues, it updated its Health app to include period tracking and added a reachability feature to temporarily shift phone displays for easier access. With more diverse teams, Apple might have designed software to meet those needs from the beginning.

Facial recognition software has repeatedly revealed the risks of neglecting diversity. Software for HP webcams came with a feature intended to keep users centered on the screen by tracking their position. It failed on dark-skinned users because it relied on a significant contrast between user's eye color and skin tone. The issue, which wasn't caught until after the product launched, would have been identified immediately if the product had been tested on users with dark skin tones.

The issue isn't unique to HP. Facial recognition software fails about 10 times more often on photos of dark-skinned women than light-skinned women, probably because the image set used to train facial recognition software is 78 percent male and 83 percent white. Google Photos ran into an even bigger problem, automatically tagging photos of some black people as gorillas or apes. At the time, only 1 percent of Google's developers

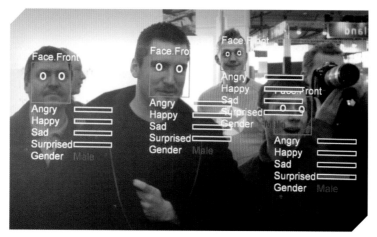

A computer screen displays the results of "Real-Time Face Detector" software, which not only identifies faces but assumes the gender and emotions of the individuals in either video or photo inputs.

were black, raising the question of whether a more diverse team might have caught the embarrassing and offensive problem before it made national news.

Facial recognition software performs badly with Asian faces as well. Richard Lee, a New Zealander of Asian descent, went viral in 2016 with his failed attempts to upload a photo to a passport application system. The software, optimized for white faces, kept wrongly insisting Lee's eyes were closed.

Gfycat, a video-hosting company, discovered similar problems when it started adapting an existing facial recognition program. During its testing process, the program often misidentified Gfycat's Asian employees. To solve the problem, the company added images of Asian people to the software training set and rewrote code to be more sensitive to Asian-specific features. Fortunately, Gfycat had a diverse team of developers, which allowed it to catch and solve the problem before users complained. Now major tech companies are racing to catch up, boosting employee diversity so they can make better products.

TACKLING BIAS

In major Silicon Valley companies, women still fill only two out of every ten technical roles. But companies have begun turning the tide by sponsoring interns, providing college scholarships, rooting out discrimination and harassment, and making sure people get equal pay for equal work.

ACTIVITY: WHO'S BEEN LEFT OUT?

Choose a video game or app you use regularly. What assumptions does it make about user's vision, hearing, and physical abilities? Does it convey any messages about age, gender, sexual orientation, or ethnicity that might make some users feel less welcome or able to use the technology?

Google invested $265 million on diversity efforts between 2014 and 2017, and Intel has committed $300 million to having a representative workforce by 2020. Slack, which makes team collaboration tools, tripled the number of people from underrepresented groups in technical roles by revamping its hiring process. Changes included rewording job descriptions to appeal to a broad audience, recruiting women and people of color through coding boot camps, and ensuring unbiased reviews of applicant's coding skills.

GapJumpers, a diversity consulting company, helps tech companies boost diversity by arranging "blind" assessments of each job applicant's work. The approach evolved out of the method that orchestras use to evaluate musicians. Years ago, when musicians auditioned directly in front of interview panels, women had difficulty getting hired. Once orchestras starting having musicians audition behind a screen, gender discrimination couldn't play a role and more women were hired. GapJumpers uses a similar technique, making sure coding skill assessments are scored by people who do not know the candidate's age, sex, ethnicity, or educational background. When raters' biases and assumptions can't influence the evaluation, 60 percent of top scorers come from underrepresented backgrounds.

Colleges have also taken steps to increase diversity. University of California, Berkeley, revamped its introductory computer science class to emphasize the meaningful impact of software on the world. The new class, The Beauty and Joy of Computing, enrolled more women than men. Harvey Mudd College, which specializes in training engineers and scientists, created an introductory programming course for true beginners and redesigned its curriculum to focus on creative problem-solving. Within a few years, the program went from having very few women majoring in computer science to being 40 percent female.

Nonprofit organizations are also working to bring more women and people of color into computer science. Code.org designed a new Advanced Placement class called

Three participants in Girls Who Code collaborate on a project. Girls Who Code offers camps, programs, and courses in cities across the United States, including New York City; Atlanta, Georgia; Los Angeles, California; and Austin, Texas.

Computer Science Principles, which focuses on creativity and critical thinking. Since the class launched in 2016, the number of girls, Latinx students, and black students taking an AP computer science class has more than doubled.

Girls Who Code, founded by attorney Reshma Saujani, offers free coding clubs for young students, intensive boot camps for high school students, and community-building programs for college women. To give equal access regardless of financial backgrounds, the seven-week boot camp is free and offers scholarships to cover transportation costs and living expenses. Girls Who Code participants (over 90,000 so far) go on to major in computer science at 15 times the national rate.

Kimberly Bryant founded Black Girls Code because her daughter was the only black girl in a sea of white, male faces at a computer science camp. "I wanted to create something where she could find another community of girls like her who were interested in technology," said Bryant. With funding from such major companies as Google and Lyft, Black Girls Code offers everything from coding workshops to career panels. The organization intends to train one million girls by 2040.

Many organizations exist to support older students, such as #YesWeCode, which gives low-income youth scholarships for tech-related education. Code2040 connects Black and Latinx college students with tech companies through tours and intensive summer fellowship programs. In Northern California, Hack the Hood teaches low-income youth of color the web development, marketing, and networking skills they need to become entrepreneurs. Participants leave the program with a portfolio of real websites they have designed for local businesses. The community benefits too, because small businesses get free, high-quality websites they wouldn't have been able to afford otherwise.

In 2017 Hack the Hood served 335 youth, delivering 48,000 hours of community service and producing 250 websites. Many of those students faced significant disadvantages in their lives—about half had a mental health diagnosis, 42 percent were living below the poverty level, and 39 percent grew up in homes where English wasn't the primary language.

For Nhat Ho, the experience was life-changing. Ho's Vietnamese parents had been prisoners of war for eight years following the Vietnam War (1957–1975). They were captured after fighting on the side of the United States. They came to the US for a better life but lived surrounded by violence, drugs, and gangs. "All my brothers work two jobs," said Ho in an interview with CNN, "and all my sisters work all day from 9 to 7 at a nail salon." To find a new path, Ho applied to Hack the Hood. After building websites for several businesses, Ho enrolled at the University of California–Davis, making him the first person in his family to attend college.

Although disparities still exist in the tech world, developers such as Ho are part of the changing face of software development. Tech companies recognize that diverse teams build better software and have invested hundreds of millions of dollars to expand opportunities for people from underrepresented groups. When people from underrepresented groups become developers, they don't have to navigate the tech world on their own. Large companies such as Microsoft and Google have employee network groups to support women, people of color, and members of the LGBTQ+ community. Developers working at smaller companies can find support through professional organizations such as the National Center for Women & Information Technology, the American Indian Science and Engineering Society, or Out in Science, Technology, Engineering, and Mathematics.

CHAPTER 8
WHAT LIES AHEAD?

By the age of 17, Sreya Guha had already created two serious apps. The first app she created makes it easy to find presidential speeches on any topic. Users enter terms such as *jobs*, *crime*, or *space exploration* at the website pres-search.appspot.com. The app returns a bar graph showing how many speeches each president gave on the topic along with links to each speech.

The second app she created helps people figure out whether claims made by a website check out. Users just paste a link into the search box at RelatedFactChecks.org and Guha's tool returns relevant fact-checks on anything from an anti-vaccination article to a political scandal. For her work on that app, Guha won the 2017 ACM/CSTA Cutler-Bell Prize in High School Computing, which comes with a $10,000 college scholarship.

Stories such as Guha's can be intimidating, making it seem as if only coding-obsessed child prodigies can become developers. But Guha wasn't born magically able to code—it took her years to build her skills. Students at her school started learning to code in seventh grade, and Guha spent four summers doing coding-related internships. Even with all that training, she still needs expert advice, turning to her teachers and software-developer father when she's stuck.

Guha's story also defies the stereotype that developers spend all their time coding. As she describes herself, "My interests include computer science, history, and convincing my parents that it's not too late to get a puppy. I love tiramisu, dosa, and Mindy Kaling." When she isn't coding, she dances and volunteers with elementary school kids.

As Guha's story shows, all kinds of people become developers. Some start coding as children, and others write their first line of code well after their hair has turned gray. Some developers love coding for coding's sake, and others see code as a useful tool for solving the world's problems. Regardless of a person's background or interests, a spot exists for them in the wide world of coding.

HELP WANTED

In October 2018, Amazon had openings for 110 data scientists, 29 database administrators, 292 user interface designers, 306 machine-learning specialists, 1,490 information technology professionals, 5,767 software developers, 1,394 software architects, and 538 network engineers.

Those openings reflect the broader job market—demand for software developers is high. That high demand translates to high salaries. In 2017 half of all developers in the United States had salaries above $102,000 (about $50,000 higher than median wages across all fields of work).

Demand for developers is also growing. According to the Bureau of Labor Statistics, the number of computer and information technology jobs will grow by about 13 percent between 2016 and 2026, adding a half-million jobs to the market.

Currently, US students majoring in computer science will fill only about 17 percent of the 3.5 million job openings expected by 2026. Top companies already need to recruit developers from around the world to meet demand. In 2017 Google and Microsoft alone filed 5,282 applications to hire developers from outside the United States.

Although demand for all types of developers is high, some specialties are growing especially quickly. Developers able to create artificial intelligence programs, write code for internet-connected devices, or prevent unauthorized data access will be in especially high demand.

ARTIFICIAL INTELLIGENCE

Experts expect rapid growth in jobs related to artificial intelligence. An AI is a decision-making program capable of tasks that usually require human intelligence, perception, or judgment. A strong AI is capable of abstract thinking, learning without human input, and solving unfamiliar problems. Perhaps someday, a strong AI will even become self-aware, capable of understanding humans and itself.

Thus far, even the most powerful AI programs fall in the weak AI category, handling specific, limited tasks such as making movie recommendations, playing chess, or translating text into another language. We have already woven AI systems into the

A rescue robot undergoes a test at the 17th International Joint Conference on Artificial Intelligence in Seattle, Washington in 2001, in which it successfully locates a dummy representing a disaster victim.

fabric of everyday life, relying on them to power digital assistants, control video game characters, determine pricing on ride-sharing apps, detect credit card fraud, and tag people in photos.

Despite the name, "weak" AI systems also have the power to save lives. Each year, disasters kill a million people and seriously injure millions more. Rapid responses save lives, but many survivors are trapped in places too small or dangerous for rescue personnel. Rescue robots can find survivors, pinpoint weak points in collapsing buildings, and identify escape routes.

Researcher Robin Murphy and her colleagues have deployed robots around the world in response to earthquakes, hurricanes, volcanic eruptions, wildfires, mine collapses, and mudslides. They don't build the robots—they craft the AI programs that allow robots to independently choose their path, change their shape, and navigate obstacles. Using those abilities, Murphy's robots have traveled through fire, floods, and rubble to collect crucial information for search and rescue teams.

Surprisingly, the main challenge facing the field of disaster robotics isn't building clever machines to get into tight spaces. Murphy explains, "The biggest problem is not making the robots smaller. It's not making them more heat resistant. It's not making more sensors. The biggest problem is the data." During emergencies, disaster robots and drones generate mountains of data. Transmitting that data swamps wireless networks, leading to delays as emergency workers hand-deliver data files and waste hours sifting through them for useful information. These information dumps overwhelm "people trying to get that one nugget of information they need to make the decision that's going to make the difference," says Murphy. To solve that problem,

Murphy is developing AI programs able to identify the most essential data to send to each emergency team.

Whether developers hope to improve disaster response or create more realistic video game characters, AI has a role to play. Experts predict an increase in AI-related openings for scientists, machine-learning specialists, statisticians, and developers. Some jobs will focus on using machine learning to train programs. Other jobs will focus on creating advanced AI programs able to train themselves. The growth of AI will also create new jobs for people in nontechnical roles, such as project managers, ethics experts, and sales and marketing professionals.

FRIENDLY AI

Self-driving cars controlled by AI systems are expected to take over our roads within the next few decades. Companies have started exploring design decisions to help people feel more comfortable with driverless cars. Jaguar Land Rover has tested a self-driving car with googly eyes that track moving objects. Research Manager Pete Bennett says, "It's second-nature to glance at the driver of the approaching vehicle before stepping into the road." Designers hope googly eyes will re-create that experience, allowing pedestrians to feel comfortable crossing in front of the car. To bridge the human to AI divide, other companies have experimented with cars that smile or talk to pedestrians.

INTERNET OF THINGS

Almost any physical object can be equipped with sensors and connected to the internet. At home, people can control smoke detectors, doorbells, lights, and appliances from their phones. Patients with serious diseases can wear, embed, or even swallow sensors that continuously monitor everything from medication levels to blood oxygenation. On the go, Apple Watch can detect falls, bike accidents, and car crashes, contacting emergency services if necessary. In cities, web-connected sensors reveal open parking spaces and overflowing trash cans and allow utility companies to identify failing equipment before it causes blackouts. In the country, soil monitors allow farmers to save money and boost productivity by identifying which parts of the field need water or fertilizer.

Together, these objects make up the rapidly growing *Internet of Things (IoT)*, the collection of physical devices able to connect to the internet or to one another. In 2016 there were over 6.3 billion connected devices. By 2020 experts expect to see more than 20 billion IoT devices, all bringing opportunities for developers with them. The IoT is driving demand for developers because each IoT device needs a user-friendly app along with firmware, the embedded software that runs the device and connects it to other devices. Developers will also play a role in integrating devices with one another. In future homes, smart refrigerators may order groceries that will be packed by robots and delivered by drones. For that to happen, developers will need to write programs that coordinate communication between devices made by different manufacturers and owned by different people.

A demonstrator shows how to communicate with an LG smart fridge via a cell phone app.

IoT ACCESSIBILITY

Digital assistants such as Google Assistant, Amazon's Alexa, and Apple's Siri allow people to control thousands of IoT devices. With simple voice commands, people can turn on lights or coffee makers, order groceries, raise the room temperature, unlock the front door for guests, stream YouTube videos, run web searches, and check online calendars for appointments.

For people with limited physical mobility, voice-controlled digital assistants have life-changing potential. However, many injuries and disorders that limit movement also impact people's ability to speak clearly, making it difficult for digital assistants to understand their commands. Because most of the input used to train voice-controlled devices comes from young, abled users, the problem will not solve itself. To help digital assistants fulfill their potential, Voiceitt has begun developing new speech recognition technology for people unable to speak clearly. Over 10 million people in the United States and Europe alone have speech disabilities, suggesting a real need for more accessible tech.

The IoT brings the promise of *smart homes,* homes filled with computer-controlled devices such as sprinkler systems that self-regulate based on weather reports and security systems that automatically lock doors and turn on lights when they detect suspicious activity. However, each new internet-connected device also offers another vulnerability for hackers to exploit. A house full of interconnected lights, garage door openers, and stereo systems makes it easy for someone with system access to know when the house is empty. That access would also allow them to disable security cameras and break in by unlocking the internet-connected front door.

Hackers can also hijack the vast IoT to attack other targets. In the 2016 Mirai botnet attack, hackers took control of over 600,000 internet-connected devices, such as security cameras and routers. They harnessed the combined power of these devices to launch a DDoS attack against a company that links human-friendly website names with their actual numeric addresses. Without that address-matching service, internet traffic in Europe and the United States slowed to a crawl. People couldn't access major websites such as Amazon, CNN, Netflix, Twitter, PayPal, Comcast, Spotify, and Pinterest. The growing IoT translates directly to a need for more security experts.

SECURITY

In the digital world, the careless or criminal acts of just a few people can wreak havoc. The Mirai botnet, which disrupted internet use around the world, wasn't created by evil geniuses but by three bungling Minecraft fans.

Although most people just play Minecraft for fun, entrepreneurs running customized Minecraft servers can make $100,000 each month. Knocking a competitor's server offline makes it easy to steal customers, so some unscrupulous people pay for illegal booter services—services that boot a rival's server off-line by flooding it with traffic.

Gamers Josiah White, Paras Jha, and Dalton Norman created Mirai to take down Minecraft servers and a company that protected Minecraft servers against booter attacks. When Mirai started knocking major companies off-line, the trio realized they'd created a monster. To cover their tracks, they released their code online, hoping widespread access to the Mirai code would make it hard to prove they'd created it.

WHAT COLOR HAT?

Some hackers break the law, but others work for law enforcement organizations. Names for different types of hackers draw on costumes from old westerns, which featured bad guys in black hats and heroes in white ones.

- **Black hat hackers** write malware and break into systems for personal gain. Whether they focus on making money, getting revenge, having fun, or stealing information, their actions cause harm to others.
- **White hat hackers** are security specialists, paid to find software vulnerabilities. Major tech companies such as Google and Microsoft offer rewards to anyone who discovers and reports a security issue.
- **Gray hat hackers** break into systems without permission but then offer to sell the company information about how they did it. Sometimes, if the company won't pay, they sell the information to someone willing to exploit that vulnerability, moving them into black hat territory.

Sharing the code only made thing worse, leading to a cascade of attacks around the world. It also failed to confuse the FBI, which quickly arrested the group.

Unfortunately, the availability of powerful hacking tools means that even people with limited coding skills can cause serious problems. Accessing a company's secure data can be as simple as tricking one employee into revealing a password or opening an infected file. In 2017 alone, companies paid $2 billion in ransom to regain access to encrypted files and lost $9 billion in email scams. Corporate hacks don't just hurt companies. They also hurt customers by exposing their personal data and putting them at risk for identity theft.

Security experts have to be aware of threats from hackers, which take a digital form, and from traditional thieves, who might use trickery to get physical access to computers.

In 2017 Equifax, one of the three major credit-reporting companies created to store people's credit histories, failed to install an essential security patch. Hackers took advantage, stealing 143 million people's personal information, including Social Security numbers, addresses, birth dates, and driver's license numbers. Many people responded by freezing their credit, hoping to keep criminals from opening credit cards in their name.

In 2018 Experian, another credit-reporting company, made matters worse by exposing the secret codes required to unfreeze a person's credit. Experian's login process was supposed to confirm people's identities by making sure they could answer personal questions correctly. However, instead of requiring correct answers, the site granted access to anyone selecting "none of the above" for each question. Experian's sloppy security led consumer advocate Mike Litt to ask, "How do you just leave the keys to the door on top of the welcome mat?"

Obviously, developers responsible for the security failures didn't intend to put people at risk. Getting cybersecurity right is hard. Just setting up a simple login requires developers to make good decisions about password requirements, create password retrieval options that help users without exposing useful information to hackers,

APPSEC

Developers can keep hackers at bay by following basic application security standards, which cover everything from data encryption to procedures for automatically signing out inactive users. Top AppSec threats include these:

- **Injection.** Without proper safeguards, hackers can inject dangerous commands through interfaces such as a website's search box.
- **Broken authentication.** If developers set up login procedures incorrectly, hackers can gain control of people's identities.
- **Broken access control.** If developers grant too much power to app users, hackers can view sensitive files, modify data, or access administrative functions with an ordinary account.
- **Sensitive data exposure.** If developers fail to encrypt data, hackers can steal or modify information.
- **Security misconfiguration.** Weak security settings and out-of-date security patches make it easy for hackers to exploit known security vulnerabilities.
- **Insufficient monitoring.** Failure to log and monitor suspicious events makes it hard to detect hacking attempts.

determine when to lock accounts for too many login failures, and ensure inactive users will be automatically logged out.

Because protecting data from unauthorized access is hard and hacking attempts are common, demand for security-focused developers is high. Security starts at the network level, where network engineers create firewalls to prevent unauthorized access and use intrusion detection systems to monitor networks for suspicious activity. These systems scan for malware, monitor suspicious changes in user permissions, and flag unusual activity, such as a sudden surge in logins from the other side of the world.

Penetration testers test system security by attempting to break into apps or a network. They explore every angle, from poor network configuration to software vulnerabilities to naive employees who open infected email attachments. When hackers strike, intrusion analysts jump into action, helping to identify the source of an attack and

limit the damage done. After an attack, forensics experts work to identify the malware and hackers responsible for the attack.

Many software engineers develop application security (AppSec) expertise, designing code to protect users and program data from external threats. Some specialists dive deeper into security work, creating antivirus software or intrusion-detection programs. Developers who also have strong math backgrounds can pursue *cryptography* careers, designing new encryption strategies to protect data against unauthorized access by converting it into a code.

Although demand for all types of cybersecurity experts is growing, demand is especially high for developers with expertise about blockchain—a relatively new approach to maintaining secure records.

BLOCKCHAIN

Imagine the chaos a hacker could create by altering or deleting bank records, police reports, or school transcripts. Organizations protect their information by monitoring signs of intrusion and backing records up in multiple locations. Still, most important records are held by single organizations in a fixed number of locations, leaving data vulnerable to attack.

Developers are tackling that problem with blockchains, which decentralize data storage by sharing information across a vast network of computers. Each "block" in a blockchain holds digital records of transactions, such as bank deposits or end-of-term academic grades. Besides having its own unique identifier, every block also stores the identifier of the previous block, stringing blocks together in a virtual chain.

Every computer in a blockchain network stores a copy of the entire blockchain. Because hackers cannot simultaneously access thousands of computers scattered around the world, blockchains create an unhackable record of events. "Blockchain is a highly processed thing," explains security expert Don Tapscott, "sort of like a Chicken McNugget. And if you wanted to hack it, it'd be like turning a Chicken McNugget back into a chicken."

Blockchain technology was introduced in 2008 to serve as a ledger for *bitcoin,* the world's first major cryptocurrency. *Cryptocurrencies* are digital forms of currency that use encryption techniques to track ownership of funds and prevent counterfeiting. The blockchain technology supporting bitcoin uses a network of linked computers to record bitcoin transactions, so a bank doesn't need to track people's accounts. As companies

SOCIAL MEDIA INSECURITIES

In 2018 alone, security risks affected users of virtually every major social media app, including the following:

- An error in Facebook's code gave hackers access to personal information from 30 million accounts. In a separate issue, Facebook accidentally gave 1,500 third-party apps access to the private photos of 6.8 million users.
- Russian hackers gained control of hundreds of Instagram accounts, changing the associated usernames, emails, and passwords to keep the real account owners locked out.
- Hackers used a false login page to dupe 55,000 Snapchat users into sharing their username and passwords. That pales in comparison to 2014, when hackers posted partial account information for 4.6 million Snapchat users to draw attention to the app's weak security.
- An undetected bug in Twitter's code gave developers access to some people's private direct messages for over a year. Twitter also accidentally stored users' passwords in plain text rather than in encrypted form.

have begun exploring other possible uses of blockchains, demand for blockchain developers has grown rapidly. Developers are already investigating ways to use blockchain to improve food safety, document home ownership, protect health records, and even help refugees verify their identities.

Unfortunately, blockchains can have an environmental downside. Maintaining the bitcoin blockchain requires such immense computing power that the computers involved used as much power in 2018 as the entire country of Switzerland. A single blockchain transaction uses enough energy to power 15 American homes for a day. Newer approaches to maintaining blockchains are more energy efficient, but the field still needs innovators to find ways to get the benefits of blockchains without harming the environment.

WHY WAIT?

Most professions require people to earn at least a college degree before they start working—high school students can't take a crack at designing buildings or prosecuting criminals. Many states won't even license people under the age of 18 to cut hair.

The normal rules don't apply to software development—a person's coding skills matter more than their age or degree. High schoolers can take classes, attend coding camps, or learn from books and online tutorials. They can also start using their skills right away by participating in hackathons, contributing to open-source projects, or developing their own apps.

Many teenagers have written code that make a real difference. Some tackle serious business problems by working with experienced developers. For example, as a summer intern at IBM, Karthik Rao worked on a flight-mapping program that used GPS and weather data to find fuel-efficient routes for airplanes. Cutting fuel consumption helps airlines save money and protects the environment. High school student Valerie Chen apprenticed with the Naval Research Laboratory where she helped develop a testing tool to detect errors in embedded software. Tackling the issue is crucial, because software problems cost the navy nearly $60 billion each year.

Other teenagers have created apps to address problems adults have overlooked. Sixteen-year-old Cherry Zou decided to tackle the link between cyberbullying and suicide by targeting anonymous bullying. She wrote a program able to identify the owners of fake social media accounts based on their writing style. In Mumbai, India, a group of girls decided to do something about the many hours girls and women wait in line to collect water. They created a Paani, a virtual line app. Instead of standing in line, girls can work, study, or play, knowing the app will alert them when their turn comes.

Clearly, the world has no shortage of opportunities for creating change, big and small. Anyone with coding skills has the power to make a difference. Why wait to get started?

ANSWER KEY

ACTIVITY ANSWER [PAGE 50]

Most songs alternate between verses, which have the same melody but different words, and the chorus, which has the same words and melody each time. For a three-verse song, the computer would need to store two melodies and four sets of lyrics.

SONG ORDER	LYRICS	MELODY
Verse 1	Lyric set 1	Melody 1
Chorus	Lyric set 2	Melody 2
Verse 2	Lyric set 3	Melody 1
Chorus	Lyric set 2	Melody 2
Verse 3	Lyric set 4	Melody 1
Chorus	Lyric set 2	Melody 2

A program could re-create this song with a loop that played a verse plus chorus, going up by one verse each time and stopping after the third repeat of the chorus.

ACTIVITY ANSWER [PAGE 62]

Partial Toothbrushing Algorithm

5. Stand facing the bathroom sink, close enough to touch the handles.

6. Open the drawer holding the toothbrush and toothpaste.

7. Use your right hand to pick up the toothpaste tube. Unscrew the cap by turning it counterclockwise with your left hand.

8. Put the toothpaste lid down.

9. Use your left hand to pick up the toothbrush by the handle, bristles facing up.

10. Move the opening of the toothpaste tube so that it almost touches the bristles.

11. Squeeze the tube hard enough to release 1/3 inch (0.8 cm) of toothpaste onto the bristles.

12. Stop squeezing.

13. Put toothpaste tube down.

14. Turn on the cold-water faucet with your right hand by turning it clockwise.

15. Pass the toothpaste-coated bristles through the stream of water, toothpaste side up.

16. Turn off the cold-water faucet with your right hand by turning it counterclockwise.

17. Pass the toothbrush from your left hand to your right hand, holding it only by the handle.

18. ...

Designing algorithms requires thinking about every step. This sample takes 13 steps just to prepare the toothbrush. If one step is missing or unclear, people will end up stuck in front of a closed drawer or spitting toothpaste onto the floor.

ACTIVITY ANSWER [PAGE 63]

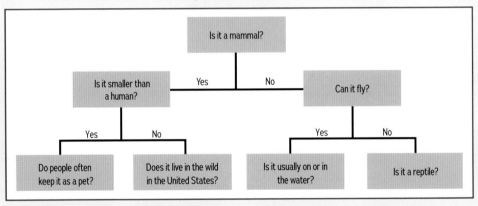

ACTIVITY ANSWER [PAGE 115]

To train an AI to spot fake news, feed the program millions of fake news stories on all topics (for example, politics, celebrities, and miracle cures) plus legitimate stories on those topics. Include opinion pieces and satires, since the program should not lump them in with fake news. In addition to the text of the article, an article's headline, publisher, or even reader comments may help an AI identify bogus stories.

TIMELINE

1801   Joseph Marie Jacquard invents a programmable loom capable of weaving elaborate patterns based on directions stored in punched cards.

1822   Charles Babbage designs an 8,000-part "analytical engine," the precursor to modern computers.

1843   Ada Lovelace publishes directions for programming Babbage's analytical engine, making her the world's first programmer.

1928   IBM designs punch cards for entering binary computer programs.

1941   English scientist Alan Turing develops the first code-breaking computer, crucial to helping Allied forces defeat Germany in World War II.

1943   Scientists create the room-sized ENIAC computer. Female mathematicians program it to perform the advanced calculus required to calculate missile-firing solutions.

1952   Former naval officer Grace Hopper creates the first compiler, a tool translating user-friendly programming languages into machine-readable code.

Doctoral student Alexander Douglas writes one of the world's first computer games, a version of tic-tac-toe called *OXO*. Players made moves using a rotary telephone dial.

1956   Dartmouth College hosts the first artificial intelligence conference.

1965   The first computer small enough to fit on a table retails for $18,000.

1969   ARPANET, the precursor to the internet, goes online with the first host-to-host connection.

1975   Atari releases the home console version of Pong, the first widely available video game. IBM releases the first desktop computer, the IBM 5100, complete with a monitor and keyboard.

Bill Gates and Paul Allen found Microsoft.

1976   Steve Jobs and Steve Wozniak found Apple.

1982   For the Man of the Year, *Time* magazine selects "computers."

1985   Microsoft releases the first version of the Windows operating system.

1997   IBM's Deep Blue computer, a sophisticated chess-playing AI, beats world chess champion Garry Kasparov.

1998   Larry Page and Sergey Brin found Google.

1999   Around the world, companies and governments spend millions to solve the Y2K bug, caused by programs that allocated only two digits to storing the year.

2002	Stores start stocking the Roomba robot vacuum, which uses a cleaning algorithm to vacuum independently.
2004	Anonymous, a major hacktivist group, goes public.
2006	Dictionaries add *google* as a verb.
	Social media goes big with the launch of Twitter and Facebook's decision to allow anyone over the age of 13 to join.
2007	Apple releases the iPhone, the world's first smartphone, ushering in a wave of mobile app development.
2008	Google begins developing self-driving cars.
2010	IBM's Watson computer uses sophisticated language analysis to beat two of the best-ever *Jeopardy* players.
	The Stuxnet virus attacks Iranian nuclear enrichment facilities, slowing Iran's progress toward nuclear weapons.
	Instagram launches.
2011	Apple introduces Siri, the first voice-activated digital assistant in widespread use.
	Snapchat launches.
2015	Image-recognition AIs surpass human object-identifying abilities in over a thousand categories.
2018	Waymo launches a self-driving taxi service in Phoeniz, AZ.
2019	AI programs can beat professional gamers in complex, strategy-based video games.

GLOSSARY

algorithm: an ordered set of directions for carrying out a task or solving a problem

application: a software program running on a computer, smartphone, or on the web that was designed for a specific function such as word processing or playing a game

application-programming interface (API): code that connects two pieces of software, allowing them to exchange information

artificial intelligence (AI): a computer system capable of tasks that usually require human intelligence, perception, reasoning, or judgment

compiler: a program that translates programs written in high-level, human-friendly languages into machine code a computer can understand

computational thinking: the problem-solving process that supports software design, including recognizing crucial aspects of problems, identifying similarities across problems, breaking large problems into small ones, and solving problems with a series of ordered steps

data: any information processed or stored by a computer

database: a collection of data, ideally structured to be easy to access and update

debugging: identifying and fixing problems in code

digital divide: the gap between people with good access to computers, the internet, and technology-related education and those who are shut out due to cultural or economic factors

distributed denial-of-service (DDoS) attack: an attack designed to shut down a computer, network, or website by using multiple systems to flood it with more information or requests than it can handle

encryption: converting data to an unrecognizable form to prevent unauthorized access

function: a named unit of code that performs a specific task

hacking: using digital tools to illegally access to a computer, network, or data set

hardware: the touchable parts of a computer system, such as keyboards, monitors, and everything inside a computer case or smartphone

integrated development environment (IDE): a tool that makes software development easier by combining editing tools, compilers, debuggers, and backup management in one place

Internet of Things (IoT): the collection of physical devices able to connect to the internet or to one another, such as smart watches, networked smoke detectors, and traffic sensors

library: a programming language-specific collection of code for developers to reuse

machine learning: a branch of artificial intelligence in which programs trained on massive data sets "learn" to recognize patterns and classify information

malware: code intended to perform damaging or unwanted behaviors. It is short for malicious software.

open-source software: programs based on code that other developers are welcome to use or modify, usually created collaboratively and given away for free

operating system (OS): the software required for basic computing functions, such as managing hardware, handling information processing and storage, and running other programs

server: a computer configured to manage network resources and provide data to other computers

software: any digitally stored program that instructs a computer to carry out specific tasks

syntax: the language-specific rules for writing code, the grammar dictating proper word order and punctuation

user experience design (UX): making software as simple and intuitive as possible, from the pathways users follow to complete tasks to the layout of individual screens

user interface design (UI): making the parts of programs that users see attractive and easy to understand

validation: ensuring developers are creating the right software, with the functions users expect

variable: a container that defines and holds information a program needs to store. It may contain text, numbers, or true-false values.

verification: testing to identify and remove coding errors

SOURCE NOTES

4   Andrea Gonzales and Sophie Houser, *Girl Code: Gaming, Going Viral, and Getting It Done* (New York: Harper, 2017), 10.

5   Gonzales and Houser, 52.

24   Max Kanat-Alexander, *Code Simplicity: The Fundamentals of Software* (Sebastopol, CA: O'Reilly Media, 2012), 55.

25   Martin Fowler, "Refactoring: Doing Design after the Program Runs," September 1998, https://martinfowler.com/distributedComputing/refactoring.pdf.

27   Steve McConnell, *Code Complete: A Practical Handbook of Software Construction,* 2nd ed. (Redmond, WA: Microsoft, 2004), 267.

32   Luke Stone, "Bringing *Pokémon GO* to Life on Google Cloud," Google, September 29, 2016, https://cloud.google.com/blog/products/gcp/bringing -pokemon-go-to-life-on-google-cloud.

36   "Bill Gates Quotes," AZ Quotes, accessed August 22, 2019, https://www.azquotes .com/author/5382-Bill_Gates?p=6.

37   "Yukihiro Matsumoto," *World Biographical Encyclopedia*, accessed December 20, 2018, https://prabook.com/web/yukihiro.matsumoto/354335.

37   Klint Finley, "Q & A with Yukihiro "Matz" Matsumoto, the Creator of Ruby," SiliconANGLE Media, August 31, 2011, https://siliconangle.com/2011/08/31 /qa-with-yukihiro-matz-matsumoto-the-creator-of-ruby/.

37   Alexis Adorn, "Flatiron-Procedural-Ruby," GitHub, accessed December 20, 2018, https://github.com/alexisadorn/Flatiron-Procedural-Ruby.

38   Yechiel Kalmenson, "RubyConf Is Nice: Reflections on RubyConf2017," *Rabbi on Rails* (blog), November 22, 2017, https://blog.yechiel.me/rubyconf-is-nice -dab165842db5.

38   Rod Stephens, *Beginning Software Engineering* (Indianapolis: John Wiley, 2015), 11.

39   Charles Petzold, *Code: The Hidden Language of Computer Hardware and Software* (Redmond, WA: Microsoft, 2000), 349.

39   "How to Write Hello World in Assembler under Windows," Stack Overflow, accessed August 22, 2019, https://stackoverflow.com/questions/1023593/how -to-write-hello-world-in-assembler-under-windows.

45   Aleksey Tsalolikhin, "Mars Code: Building Robust Software," Vertical Sysadmin, October 2012, http://www.verticalsysadmin.com/making_robust_software/.

51   Soumow Atitallah, "Interview with Julia Liuson, Corporate Vice President of Visual Studio and .NET," Channel 9, Microsoft, May 3, 2017, 5:30, https:// channel9.msdn.com/Shows/GALs/Interview-with-Julia-Liuson-Corporate-Vice -President-of-Visual-Studio-and-NET.

51   Atitallah.

54   Dina Katabi, "A New Way to Monitor Vital Signs (That Can See through Walls),"
      TED video, 0:33, April 2018, https://www.ted.com/talks/dina_katabi_a_new
      _way_to_monitor_vital_signs_that_can_see_through_walls/transcript.

54   Katabi, 3:37.

55   Dina Katabi, "President Obama Hosts the First-Ever White House Demo Day,"
      YouTube video, 14:45, posted by the Obama White House, August 4, 2015, https://
      www.youtube.com/watch?v=aKsxHS5vptM&feature=youtu.be.

60   Edgar Haren, "Big Data at UPS. Interview with Jack Levis," Oracle, August 4, 2017,
      https://blogs.oracle.com/database/big-data-at-ups-interview-with-jack-levis.

65   "How Search Organizes Information," Google, accessed August 23, 2019, https://
      www.google.com/search/howsearchworks/crawling-indexing/.

65   "Year in Search 2017," Google Trends, accessed December 20, 2018, https://
      trends.google.com/trends/yis/2017/GLOBAL/.

68   Tristan Harris, "How Technology Hijacks People's Minds—From a Magician and
      Google's Design Ethicist," Observer, June 1, 2016, https://observer.com/2016/06
      /how-technology-hijacks-peoples-minds%E2%80%8A-%E2%80%8Afrom-a
      -magician-and-googles-design-ethicist/.

69   Tristan Harris, "How a Handful of Tech Companies Control Billions of Minds Every
      Day," TED video, April 2017, 14:49, https://www.ted.com/talks/tristan_harris_the
      _manipulative_tricks_tech_companies_use_to_capture_your_attention/transcript.

72   Irene Au, "Design and the Self," Medium, August 10, 2016, https://medium.com
      /design-your-life/design-and-the-self-a5670a000fee.

74   Kaveh Waddell, "Why Some Apps Use Fake Progress Bars," *Atlantic*, February 21,
      2107, https://www.theatlantic.com/technology/archive/2017/02/why-some
      -apps-use-fake-progress-bars/517233/.

74   Molly McHugh, "Scotty Allen's Mom Will Judge Your Website," *Wired,* May 22,
      2015, https://www.wired.com/2015/05/theuserismymom/.

74   Scotty Allen, "The User is My Mom," December 7, 2018, https://theuserismymom
      .com.

76   Kylie Jenner, "sooo does anyone else not open Snapchat anymore? Or is it just
      me . . . ugh this is so sad," *Twitter*, February 21, 2018, https://www.change.org/p
      /snap-inc-remove-the-new-snapchat-update.

76   Will Oremus, "Is Snapchat Really Confusing, or Am I Just Old?" Slate, January 29,
      2015, https://slate.com/technology/2015/01/snapchat-why-teens-favorite-app
      -makes-the-facebook-generation-feel-old.html.

76   Hannah Alvarez, "The Generation Gap of Snapchat: UX for Different Age Groups," *UserTesting* (blog), April 21, 2015, https://www.usertesting.com/blog/snapchat/.

78   Sean Flynn, "The Real Story of the Hawaiian Missile Crisis," *GQ*, April 2, 2018, https://www.gq.com/story/real-story-of-hawaiian-missile-crisis.

78   Shannon Liao, "Hawaii's Missile Alert Interface Had a One-Word Difference between Sending a Test Alert and a Real One," Vox Media, January 16, 2018, https://www.theverge.com/2018/1/16/16896368/hawaii-false-missile-alert-system-confusing-interface-poor-design.

80   Lorrie Cranor, "Time to Rethink Mandatory Password Changes," Federal Trade Commission, March 2, 2016, https://www.ftc.gov/news-events/blogs/techftc/2016/03/time-rethink-mandatory-password-changes.

80   Lorrie Cranor, Blase Ur, Lujo Bauer, Michelle Mazurek, and Nicholas Christin, "Choose Better Passwords with the Help of Science," Conversation, August 30, 2017, https://theconversation.com/choose-better-passwords-with-the-help-of-science-82361.

82   Bill Sourour, "The Code I'm Still Ashamed Of," FreeCodeCamp, November 13, 2016, https://medium.freecodecamp.org/the-code-im-still-ashamed-of-e4c021dff55e.

82   Sourour.

83   Kate Conger, "Google Removes 'Don't Be Evil' Clause from Its Code of Conduct," Gizmodo, May 18, 2018, https://gizmodo.com/google-removes-nearly-all-mentions-of-dont-be-evil-from-1826153393.

84   Bill Bryson, *Notes from a Big Country* (Toronto: Anchor Canada), 2002, 320.

85   "Tay AI—'Tay' Went from 'Humans Are Super Cool' to Full Nazi in <24 Hrs," Know Your Meme, accessed August 23, 2019, https://knowyourmeme.com/photos/1096609-tay-ai.

88   Cathy O'Neil, *Weapons of Math Destruction: How Big Data Increases Inequality and Threatens Democracy* (New York: Crown Publishers, 2016), 3.

90   Aja Romano, "The Facebook Data Breach Wasn't a Hack. It Was a Wake-Up Call," Vox Media, March 20, 2018, https://www.vox.com/2018/3/20/17138756/facebook-data-breach-cambridge-analytica-explained.

90   Dylan Curran, "Are You Ready? Here Is All the Data Facebook and Google Have on You," *Guardian* (US edition), March 30, 2018, https://www.theguardian.com/commentisfree/2018/mar/28/all-the-data-facebook-google-has-on-you-privacy.

92   Dustin Volz, "U.S. Blames North Korea for 'WannaCry' Cyber Attack," Reuters, December 18, 2017, https://www.reuters.com/article/us-usa-cyber-northkorea/u-s-blames-north-korea-for-wannacry-cyber-attack-idUSKBN1EDO0Q.

94   "Stuxnet: Computer Worm Opens New Era of Warfare," *CBS News*, June 4, 2012, https://www.cbsnews.com/news/stuxnet-computer-worm-opens-new-era-of-warfare-04-06-2012/4/.

95   Samuel Gibbs, "Anonymous Swaps Isis Propaganda Site for Prozac Ad in Trolling Fight," *Guardian* (US edition), November 26, 2015, https://www.theguardian.com/technology/2015/nov/26/anonymous-swaps-isis-propaganda-site-for-prozac-ad-in-trolling-fight.

96   "ACM Code of Ethics and Professional Conduct," Association for Computing Machinery, June 22, 2018, https://www.acm.org/code-of-ethics.

97   Lyndsey Scott, "What's It Like Going from Bullied High-Schooler to Fashion Model?," Slate, December 27, 2013, http://www.slate.com/blogs/quora/2013/12/27/model_lyndsey_scott_on_the_benefits_of_attractiveness.html.

98   Madeline Buxton, "This Victoria's Secret Model Is Also a Coder: That Shouldn't Be Newsworthy," Refinery29, September 14, 2018, https://www.refinery29.com/en-us/2018/09/209930/lyndsey-scott-model-developer-instagram.

99   " 'Uncle' Bob Martin—The Future of Programming," YouTube video, 10:46, posted by "Expert Talks Mobile," May 18, 2016, https://www.youtube.com/watch?v=ecIWPzGEbFc&t=1528s.

102   "Internet/Broadband Fact Sheet," Pew Research Center, accessed August 22, 2019, http://www.pewinternet.org/fact-sheet/internet-broadband/.

104   Abigail Wheat,"High School Girl to College Recruiters: Don't Make Everything Pink!," *Public Radio International*, July 15, 2015, http://www.keranews.org/post/high-school-girl-college-recruiters-dont-make-everything-pink.

104   Katie Dupere, "To Let Girls In, the Tech Industry Is Thinking Pink. But That Isn't Enough," Mashable, January 24, 2016, https://mashable.com/2016/01/24/coding-girls-pink/#OgqLXL5u1EqF.

105   Liza Mundy, "Why Is Silicon Valley So Awful to Women?," *Atlantic*, April 2017, https://www.theatlantic.com/magazine/archive/2017/04/why-is-silicon-valley-so-awful-to-women/517788/.

105   bethanye Blount McKinney, User Profile, LinkedIn, accessed August 21, 2019, https://www.linkedin.com/in/bethanye/.

105   Mundy, "Silicon Valley."

106   Kate Conger, "Exclusive: Here's the Full 10 Page Anti-Diversity Screed Circulating Internally at Google [Updated]," Gizmodo, August 5, 2017, https://gizmodo.com/exclusive-heres-the-full-10-page-anti-diversity-screed-1797564320.

106   Katherine W. Phillips, "How Diversity Makes Us Smarter," *Scientific American*, October 1, 2014, https://www.scientificamerican.com/article/how-diversity-makes-us-smarter/.

107   Kathryn Minshew, "This Is What Tech's Ugly Gender Problem Really Looks Like," *Wired*, July 28, 2014, https://www.wired.com/2014/07/gender-gap/.

110   Laura Bernheim, "Imagine, Build, Create—Black Girls Code Inspires Young Women of Color to Diversify Computer Sciences Classrooms," HostingAdvice.com, May 3, 2018, https://www.hostingadvice.com/blog/black-girls-code-inspires-young-women-of-color/.

111   Natalie Angley, "Hack the Hood: Preparing Low-Income Youth for Tech Jobs," *CNN*, September 29, 2014, https://money.cnn.com/2014/09/29/smallbusiness/hack-the-hood/.

112   Sreya Guha, "A Little More about Me," *Sreya Guha* (blog), accessed December 20, 2018, http://www.sreyaguha.net/.

114   Robin Murphy, "These Robots Come to the Rescue of a Disaster," TED, May 2015, https://www.ted.com/talks/robin_murphy_these_robots_come_to_the_rescue_after_a_disaster/transcript?language=en#t-254249.

115   Jesus Diaz, "People Don't Trust Autonomous Vehicles, So Jaguar Added Googly Eyes," *Fast Company*, September 6, 2018, https://www.fastcompany.com/90231563/people-dont-trust-autonomous-vehicles-so-jaguar-is-adding-googly-eyes.

119   Liz Weston, "Experian Flaw Just Revealed PINs Protecting Credit Data," NerdWallet, October 4, 2018, https://www.nerdwallet.com/blog/finance/security-flaw-at-experian-allows-easy-access-to-pin-to-unlock-credit-freeze/.

121   "Comparing Blockchain to a Chicken Nugget—Last Week Tonight," YouTube video, 1:00, posted by Blockchain Research Institute, March 12, 2018, https://www.youtube.com/watch?time_continue=32&v=8ALmkZn_X5o.

SELECTED BIBLIOGRAPHY

Bosker, Bianca. "The Binge Breaker." *Atlantic*, November 2016. https://www.theatlantic
.com/magazine/archive/2016/11/the-binge-breaker/501122/.

Chappell, Bill. "Sexist Reactions to an Ad Spark #ILookLikeAnEngineer Campaign." *NPR*,
August 4, 2015. https://www.npr.org/sections/thetwo-way/2015/08/04/429362127
/sexist-reactions-to-an-ad-spark-ilooklikeanengineer-campaign/.

Couch, Christina. "Ghosts in the Machine." *PBS*, October 25, 2017. http://www.pbs.org
/wgbh/nova/next/tech/ai-bias/.

"The Current State of Women in Computer Science." ComputerScience.org. Accessed
August 23, 2019. https://www.computerscience.org/resources/women-in-computer-science/.

Desjardins, Jeff. "How Many Millions of Lines of Code Does It Take? Visual Capitalist,
February 8, 2017. http://www.visualcapitalist.com/millions-lines-of-code/.

Eveleth, Rose. "How Self-Tracking Apps Exclude Women." *Atlantic*, December 15, 2014.
https://www.theatlantic.com/technology/archive/2014/12/how-self-tracking-apps
-exclude-women/383673/.

Fortney, Lucas. "How Does *Fortnite* Make Money?" Dotdash, October 4, 2018. https://
www.investopedia.com/tech/how-does-fortnite-make-money/.

Funk, Cary, and Kim Parker. "Women and Men in STEM Often at Odds over Workplace Equity."
Pew Research Center, January 9, 2018. http://www.pewsocialtrends.org/2018/01/09
/women-and-men-in-stem-often-at-odds-over-workplace-equity/.

Grignull, Harry. "Types of Dark Pattern." Dark Patterns. Accessed December 20, 2018. https://
darkpatterns.org/types-of-dark-pattern. https://darkpatterns.org/types-of-dark-pattern.

Harvey, Brian. *Russian Planetary Exploration: History, Development, Legacy and Prospects*.
New York: Springer Science & Business Media, 2007.

Howe, Neil. "A Special Price Just for You." *Forbes,* November 17, 2017. https://www.forbes
.com/sites/neilhowe/2017/11/17/a-special-price-just-for-you/.

"How Search Works." Google. Accessed August 23, 2019. https://www.google.com/search
/howsearchworks/.

"Improving the User Experience." US Department of Health and Human Services. Accessed
August 23, 2019. https://www.usability.gov/.

Johnson, Phil. "RSVP Required: The Code That Drives the Mars *Curiosity* Rover." IDG
Communications, January 8, 2013. https://www.itworld.com/article/2832775/mobile/rsvp
-required--the-code-that-drives-the-mars-curiosity-rover.html.

Krigsman, Michael. "IT Failure at Heathrow T5: What Really Happened." ZDNet, April 7,
2008. https://www.zdnet.com/article/it-failure-at-heathrow-t5-what-really-happened/.

Liao, Shannon. "Hawaii's Missile Alert Interface Had a One-Word Difference between
Sending a Test Alert and a Real One." Vox Media, January 16, 2018. https://www.theverge
.com/2018/1/16/16896368/hawaii-false-missile-alert-system-confusing-interface-poor
-design.

Linik, Joyce Riha. "How Female ENIAC Programmers Pioneered the Software Industry." IQ Intel, June 29, 2016. https://iq.intel.com/how-female-eniac-programmers-pioneered-the-software-industry/.

"May 2017 National Occupational Employment and Wage Estimates." United States Department of Labor Bureau of Labor Statistics, March 30, 2018. https://www.bls.gov/oes/current/oes_nat.htm#15-0000.

Miller, Michael. *The Internet of Things: How Smart TVs, Smart Cars, Smart Homes, and Smart Cities Are Changing the World.* Indianapolis: Que, 2015.

Ming, Lo Min. "UI, UX: Who Does What? A Designer's Guide to the Tech Industry." *Fast Company*, July 7, 2014. https://www.fastcompany.com/3032719/ui-ux-who-does-what-a-designers-guide-to-the-tech-industry.

Murray, Anna. *The Complete Software Project Manager: Mastering Technology from Planning to Launch and Beyond.* Hoboken, NJ: John Wiley, 2016.

National Aeronautics and Space Administration. "Press Kit: Mars Science Laboratory Launch." NASA, November 2011. https://www.jpl.nasa.gov/news/press_kits/MSLLaunch.pdf.

Nordell, Jessica. "How Slack Got ahead in Diversity." *Atlantic,* April 26, 2018. https://www.theatlantic.com/technology/archive/2018/04/how-slack-got-ahead-in-diversity/558806/.

Petzold, Charles. *Code: The Hidden Language of Computer Hardware and Software.* Redmond, WA: Microsoft, 2000.

Simonite, Tom. "How Coders Are Fighting Bias in Facial Recognition Software." *Wired,* March 29, 2018. https://www.wired.com/story/how-coders-are-fighting-bias-in-facial-recognition-software/.

Stephens, Rod. *Beginning Software Engineering.* Indianapolis: John Wiley, 2015.

Sullivan, Danny. "How Google Autocomplete Works in Search." Google, April 20, 2018. https://www.blog.google/products/search/how-google-autocomplete-works-search/.

Tsalolikhin, Aleksey. "Mars Code: Building Robust Software." Vertical Sysadmin, October 2012. http://www.verticalsysadmin.com/making_robust_software/.

Ward, Adrian F., Kristen Duke, Ayelet Gneezy, and Maarten W. Bos. "Brain Drain: The Mere Presence of One's Own Smartphone Reduces Available Cognitive Capacity." *Journal for the Association for Consumer Research* 2, no. 2 (April 3, 2017): 140–154. https://www.journals.uchicago.edu/doi/pdfplus/10.1086/691462.

Wayner, Peter. "12 Ethical Dilemmas Gnawing at Developers Today." *InfoWorld,* April 21, 2014. https://www.infoworld.com/article/2607452/application-development/12-ethical-dilemmas-gnawing-at-developers-today.html.

Wohlsen, Marcus. "The Astronomical Math behind UPS' New Tool to Deliver Packages Faster." *Wired,* June 13, 2013. https://www.wired.com/2013/06/ups-astronomical-math/.

FURTHER INFORMATION

Books

Barry, Paul. *Head First Python, 2nd Edition: A Brain-Friendly Guide*. Sebastopol, CA: O'Reilly, 2017.

Bedell, Jane. *So, You Want to Be a Coder? The Ultimate Guide to a Career in Programming, Video Game Creation, Robotics, and More!* Hillsboro, OR: Beyond Words, 2016.

Christian, Brian, and Tom Griffiths. *Algorithms to Live By: The Computer Science of Human Decisions.* New York: Henry Holt, 2016.

Erwig, Martin. *Once upon an Algorithm: How Stories Explain Computing*. Cambridge, MA: MIT Press, 2017.

Evans, Claire. *Broad Band: The Untold Story of the Women Who Made the Internet*. New York: Penguin Random House, 2018.

Freeman, Eric. *Head First Learn to Code: A Learner's Guide to Coding and Computational Thinking*. Sebastopol, CA: O'Reilly, 2018.

Gonzales, Andrea, and Sophie Houser. *Girl Code: Gaming, Going Viral, and Getting It Done*. New York: Harper, 2017.

Help Your Kids with Computer Science: A Unique Visual Step-by-Step Guide to Computers, Coding, and Communication. New York: DK, 2018.

January, Brendan. *Information Insecurity: Privacy under Siege*. Minneapolis: Twenty-First Century Books, 2016.

McPherson, Stephanie S. *Artificial Intelligence: Building Smarter Machines*. Minneapolis: Twenty-First Century Books, 2017.

Miller, Michael. *The Internet of Things: How Smart TVs, Smart Cars, Smart Homes, and Smart Cities Are Changing the World*. Indianapolis: Que, 2015.

O'Neill, Cathy. *Weapons of Math Destruction: How Big Data Increases Inequality and Threatens Democracy*. New York: Crown, 2016.

Saujani, Reshma. *Girls Who Code: Learn to Code and Change the World*. New York: Viking, 2017.

Videos

Code: Debugging the Gender Gap. DVD. Warren, NJ: Passion River, 2016. Although there are more computer science jobs than qualified graduates to fill them, the field remains dominated by white men. This documentary explores the stereotypes, cultural factors, and barriers that have led to this imbalance.

Codegirl. DVD. Los Angeles: H Films, 2015. This documentary follows girls from Brazil, Moldova, and the United States as they design apps for an international competition.

Defeating the Hackers. BBC Documentary. YouTube video. 1:27:57. Posted by Ena Daron, September 1, 2017. https://www.youtube.com/watch?v=fTK8fqOiUdc. In this documentary, journalists explore hackers and the researchers and computer scientists determined to stop them.

The Secret Rules of Modern Living: Algorithms. DVD. London: BBC Four, 2015. Mathematics professor Marcus du Sautoy describes the many ways algorithms shape everything from what we buy to how we match transplant patients with donor organs.

We Are Legion: The Story of the Hacktivists. DVD. Los Angeles: Luminant Films, 2012. This documentary covers major hacks carried out by Anonymous, one of the largest and most famous hacktivist collectives. Some of the hacks described had clear social justice goals, while others appeared to involve personally motivated acts of revenge.

Websites

App Inventor
http://www.appinventor.org/
Free online tutorials show beginners how to create smartphone apps by connecting blocks of code.

Blockly Games
https://blockly-games.appspot.com/
Free games on this site teach key programming concepts.

Code
https://studio.code.org/courses/
Code.org teaches students how to make games, apps, and websites. They have lessons in multiple programming languages, with options for elementary school through college students.

Code Academy
https://www.codecademy.com/
This site has free introductory tutorials in web development, programming, and data science along with advanced tutorials for paid subscribers. Tutorials cover HTML/CSS, JavaScript, Python, and SQL.

Code Conquest
https://codeconquest.com/tutorials/
This free site allows students to explore multiple programming languages.

Computer Science
https://www.computerscience.org/
ComputerScience.org helps people chart their path in computer science careers. It describes careers, education options, and scholarships.

Crunchzilla
https://www.crunchzilla.com/
This free site teaches JavaScript, a language used for web browsers, through step-by-step tutorials.

CS50 AP Curriculum
https://ap.cs50.net/curriculum/
Harvard University maintains a free online advanced placement computer science curriculum. Although the website is for teachers, the video lectures, notes, and exercises are designed for high school students.

EarSketch
https://earsketch.gatech.edu/
Free lessons on this site teach students to create music by writing code. No coding or musical background is required.

Hour of Code
https://hourofcode.com/us/learn/
This site offers hundreds of free coding activities for everyone from preschoolers through high school students. As the name suggests, each lesson takes an hour or less.

Khan Academy: Computing
https://www.khanacademy.org/computing/
Khan Academy offers free video-guided coding tutorials in JavaScript, HTML/CSS, and SQL, taking users from novice level through advanced exercises. The academy also offers in-depth exercises about algorithms, cryptography, the internet, and computer hardware.

Kodu Game Lab
https://www.kodugamelab.com/
The free Kodu Game Lab lets students create games by arranging images that represent code. No typing or coding experience is necessary. Beginners can create simple games quickly. More advanced students can create elaborate game worlds.

MIT App Inventor
https://appinventor.mit.edu/explore/
Free step-by-step guides allow beginners to create smartphone apps. The site also showcases student-written apps that have had important social impacts.

SAS Insights
https://www.sas.com/en_us/insights.html
The SAS Institute, makers of analytic software, offer up-to-date information on topics including artificial intelligence, big data, security, and the Internet of Things.

Scratch

https://scratch.mit.edu/

The Massachusetts Institute of Technology created Scratch, a user-friendly visual coding language to teach people how to code games and animations. The free tool is simple enough for older elementary school students but powerful enough for high school students.

Stack Overflow

https://stackoverflow.com/

This site is the largest online community of developers. Unlike a typical discussion forum, the site focuses on questions and answers. Beginners can find answers to most of their questions with a quick search. More advanced users can ask detailed questions and get answers from experts (or even contribute their own answers).

INDEX

ABOUT THE AUTHOR

Jennifer Connor-Smith, PhD, is a clinical psychologist and writer. She got her first taste of coding in 1982 by writing a BASIC program to handle simple calculations. As a researcher investigating teen stress, she wrote code to run statistical analyses every day for over a decade. She loved teaching her students to write programs that would transform a chaotic mass of data into information about how to help people cope with problems.

Because she married a software architect, normal dinner conversation ranges from the relative merits of various database structures to the potential of blockchain. Although she knows a fair bit about how developers create video games, she can't beat her kids (or anyone else) at one.

PHOTO ACKNOWLEDGMENTS

Image credits: Slaven Vlasic/Getty Images, p. 5; Justin Sullivan/Getty Images, p. 8; Chesnot/Getty Images, p. 9; © xkcd comics, pp. 15, 28, 119; SAUL LOEB/AFP/Getty Images, p. 17; Women of Color in Tech, p. 18; NASA, p. 19; Andia/Universal Images Group/Getty Images, p. 32; XAVIER GALIANA/AFP/Getty Images, p. 35; NASA/JPL-Caltech/MSSS, p. 45; Glenn Koenig/Los Angeles Times/Getty Images, p. 52; Barry Chin/The Boston Globe/Getty Images, p. 54; photovibes/iStock/Getty Images, p. 61; © Tristan Harris, p. 68; DMEPhotography/iStock/Getty Images, p. 70; stockcam/Getty Images, p. 76; EUGENE TANNER/AFP/Getty Images, p. 78; COMiCZ/iStock/Getty Images, p. 85; Ann Hermes/Christian Science Monitor/Getty Images, p. 87; Sergei Bobylev/TASS/Getty Images, p. 88; Sam Tsang/South China Morning Post/Getty Images, p. 92; Stuart C. Wilson/Getty Images, p. 97; © Isis Anchalee, p. 98; U.S. Army Photo, p. 100; SSPL/Getty Images, p. 101; © WOC in Tech, p. 105; JOHN MACDOUGALL/AFP/Getty Images, p. 108; Girls Who Code, p. 110; Tim Matsui/Getty Images, p. 114; ROBYN BECK/AFP/Getty Images, p. 116; Photofusion/Universal Images Group/Getty Images, p. 123.

Design elements: AliseFox/istock/Getty Images, p. 1; mfto/DigitalVision Vectors/Getty Images, p. 3.

Cover images: skynesher/Getty Images; Jay Yuno/Getty Images; Caiaimage/Agnieszka Olek/Getty Images; Africa Studio/Shutterstock.com; Vit-Mar/Shutterstock.com.